JUL 3 1 2012

ELK GROVE VILLAGE PUBLIC LIBRARY

3 1250 01001 1660

17
1/12
9/12

P9-ELX-740

Discarded By Elk Grove
Village Public Library

the Flying MACHINE Book

Build and Launch 35 Rockets,
Gliders, Helicopters, Boomerangs, and More

BOBBY MERCER

CHICAGO
REVIEW
PRESS ELK GROVE VILLAGE PUBLIC LIBRARY
1001 WELLINGTON AVE
ELK GROVE VILLAGE, IL 60007
(847) 439-0447

To teachers everywhere,
Thanks for inspiring children every day.

Copyright © 2012 by Bobby Mercer
All rights reserved
First edition
Published by Chicago Review Press, Incorporated
814 North Franklin Street
Chicago, Illinois 60610
ISBN 978-1-61374-086-6

Library of Congress Cataloging-in-Publication Data
Mercer, Bobby, 1961-
  The flying machine book : build and launch 35 rockets, gliders, helicopters, boomerangs, and more / Bobby Mercer. —
1st ed.
      p. cm.
  Summary: "Shows readers how to turn rubber bands, paper clips, straws, plastic bottles, and index cards into amazing, gravity-defying flyers. Each project contains a material list and detailed step-by-step instructions with photos. Mercer also includes explanations of the science behind each flyer, including concepts such as lift, thrust, and drag, the Bernoulli effect, and more"-- Provided by publisher.
      ISBN 978-1-61374-086-6 (pbk.)
  1. Paper airplanes. 2. Flying-machines--Models. I. Title.

TL778.M47 2012
745.592—dc23

2011041174

Cover design: Andrew Brozyna
Interior design and illustrations: Scott Rattray
Interior photographs: Bobby Mercer

Printed in the United States of America
5 4 3 2 1

Contents

Acknowledgments vii

Introduction ix

1 Flight School 1

2 Rockets 7

Basic Straw Rocket 9

Cruise Missile 15

Bottle Rocket 21

Soda Pop Rocket 27

Blow Darts 30

Whisper Rocket 33

3 Hand-Powered Gliders 37

Flying Flounder 39

Plastic Zipper 41

Paper Plate Flyer 45

Red Baron 49

Round Square Flyer   51

Three-Penny Flyer   54

Phonebook Flipper   60

4 Rubber Band-Powered Gliders   65

Classic Dart   67

Flat Flyer   72

Mini-Delta Flyer   79

F-16   87

Falcon Frenzy   94

Streak   100

Foam Plate Shuttle   104

Bat-Wing Flyer   109

5 Helicopters   117

Apache   119

Straw Copter   123

Super Spinner   127

Maple Key Helicopter   134

Fantastic Four-Blade   143

6 *Launchers* 147

X-Wing Flyer and Launcher   149

Grape Bazooka   157

Straight-as-an-Arrow Launcher   164

Pistol Grip Launcher   166

Pringles Launcher   173

7 *Boomerangs* 177

Basic Fingerrang   179

Triple Threat   182

Criss-Cross Flyer   185

Ninja Star   189

Aussic   192

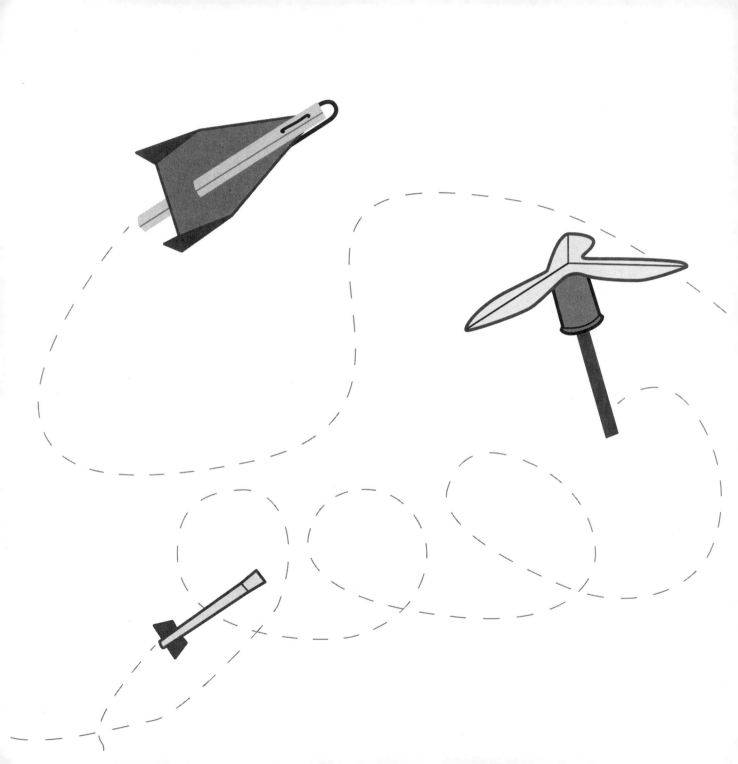

Acknowledgments

Thanks to all the people who helped turn an idea for free flying machines into this book. Kathy Green for helping this book find a home. Jerome Pohlen and the creative people at Chicago Review Press for making it look great. Robert Frost and Greg Robinson for lending me their real flying experience. But most of all, thanks to my wonderful family. Michele, you are amazing and understanding when I don't put the scissors back. Nicole, for helping me build many of the flyers in this book. Jordan, thanks for making everyone in the house smile. A special thanks to Molly, Belle, and Sally, our three lovingly psycho cats, for chasing flyers all around the house and the great outdoors.

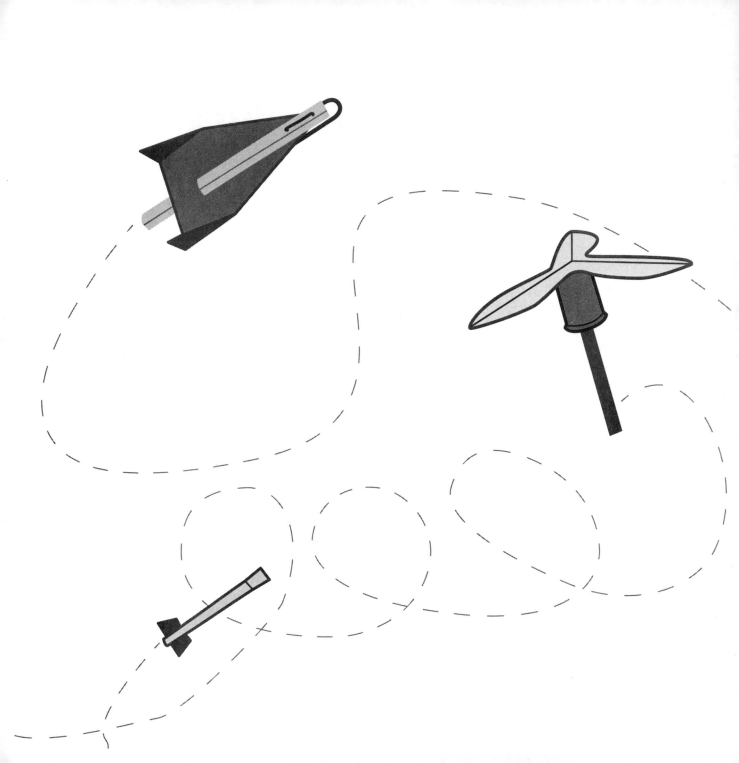

Introduction

A bird in flight is an inspiring beauty to behold. Making and flying things with your own hands is just pure fun. We have all enjoyed the feeling of watching our creations take off. Seeing paper airplanes being tossed about is a joy. Water balloons arcing gracefully toward an intended target make us smile.

The flying projects in this book range from very easy to difficult, and everybody should to be able to find a favorite. Each fun flyer project is designed to let you experiment with, tweak, and explore the wonderful world of flight. The materials required for these flyers are everyday items found in most homes and classrooms, so there is no expensive stuff to buy. Just go have fun!

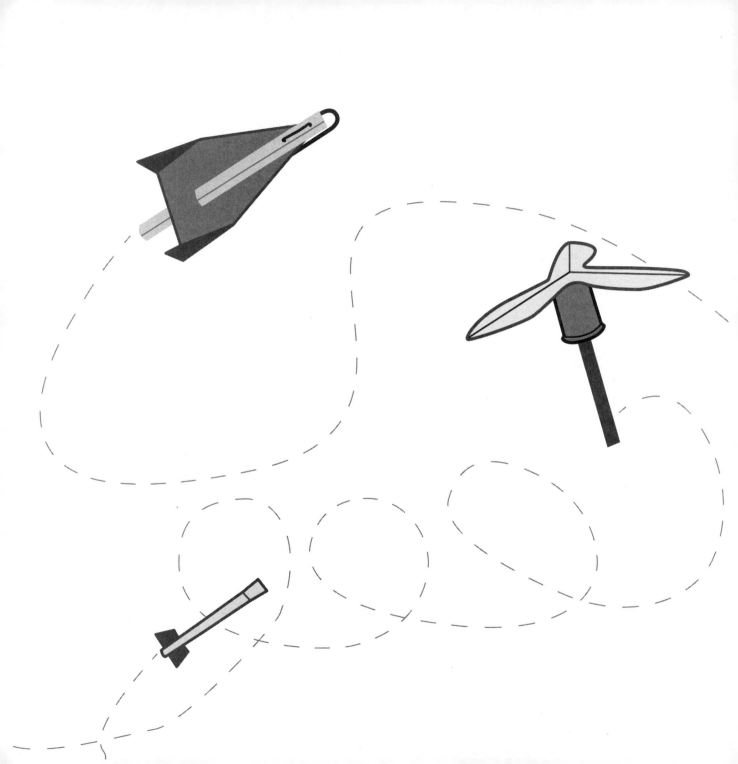

1

Flight School

The ability to fly has amazed people since time began. The earliest humans watched birds soaring in the sky and dreamed of joining them. Kites were probably humankind's first attempt to reach the skies. The Chinese first started flying kites around 400 BC, for ceremonies and just for fun.

Leonardo da Vinci was the first person known to seriously study flight. His drawings described his theories on bird flight. Da Vinci even drew pictures of imaginary flyers that would allow a person to fly under his or her own power. Although none were built for over 400 years, his designs inspired the invention of the helicopter.

In the late 1700s, hot air gave human-powered flight a lift. People discovered that hot air rises, so a bag filled with hot air will float. This led to the invention of the hot air balloon. Hot air balloons soared over Europe in the 1780s, giving people the opportunity to realize their dreams of flying through the air.

Around 1800, Englishman George Cayley took flying in a new direction when he discovered the modern airfoil. Cayley, often called the Father of Aviation because of his studies, is acknowledged as the first person to realize that the battling forces governing flight were lift, thrust, drag, and weight. He also built the first glider capable of holding a person, and that first flyer was a 10-year-old boy. Cayley also experimented with rudders and flaps, just like you will on the flyers in this book.

Of course, the Wright brothers pioneered *powered* flight, but Cayley's work is more closely related to the flying machines you will be building.

Each chapter in this book focuses on one type of flyer: helicopters, rockets, boomerangs, and different types of gliders. Not all the flyers are easy to make, and many take practice to perfect. But with a little patience, your flyer can reach the sky.

The Bernoulli Principle

Daniel Bernoulli's dad, a brilliant mathematician, never wanted his son to study math. Instead, he wanted Daniel to study medicine because it paid better. Daniel did go into medicine but never forgot his love of math. As a math professor in his 20s, he discovered a principle that combined his interests in math, science, and medicine, and it made him both famous and rich.

At the time of his discovery, Bernoulli was working with blood. He wanted to know about the relationship between blood pressure inside an artery and the speed of the blood through the artery. He soon realized that if he punctured a tube carrying a fluid with a thin pipe, the fluid would go up the pipe. And more interestingly, how far it rose (due to pressure) was related to the speed of the fluid past the end of the pipe. For the next 150 years in Europe, physicians would measure blood pressure by piercing a patient's artery with a thin glass tube. Luckily for you and me, we have a safer way to measure blood pressure today.

Even though Bernoulli was working with a liquid, the same principle works for gases such as air. Scientists classify both liquids and gases as fluids, since they flow.

You can see Bernoulli's principle at work by doing this simple experiment. Hold a long strip of paper (a dollar bill works well) tucked tightly just under your bottom lip. Blow hard, directly outward, and the strip will rise. Fast-moving air creates a low pressure above the paper, and the strip lifts.

Now, let's put Bernoulli's principle to work and learn more about the science of flight.

Four Forces

Flight is governed by four forces: lift, thrust, drag, and weight.

Lift

Thanks to Mr. Bernoulli, we now know that as air moves over an airfoil (airplane wing, helicopter rotor blade, etc.), the air over the top has to travel a greater distance. Because it travels a greater distance in the same amount of time, it moves faster than the air moving under the wing. Faster air has lower pressure than slower air. High pressure under the wing will lift the wing up toward the area of lower pressure.

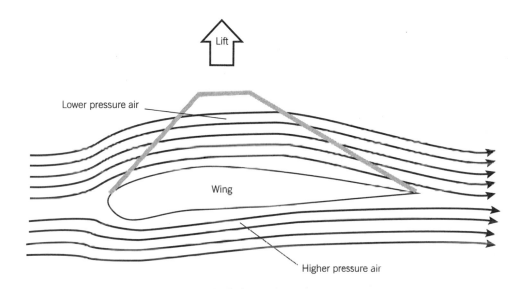

Thrust

Thrust comes from the engine on most traditional airplanes, or from the rocket engine on a rocket. Thrust causes the plane to fly forward. However, since you won't be using engines in this book, your flying machines' thrust will come from other sources. You will use muscle power and stretched rubber bands for most of your flyers. After you launch a flyer, only inertia keeps the flyer moving forward.

Moving things want to stay moving. **Inertia** is the resistance to change in motion. One example of inertia is when your body goes forward on a bus as the bus slows to a stop. Inertia will keep your flyer going until air friction (drag) causes it to slow. Since inertia depends upon the mass of an object, you will often add small weights, such as pennies and paper clips, to help keep your flyers going.

Drag

Thrust and drag wage a constant battle as flyers soar. **Drag** is friction from the air. As a flyer moves through the air, it pushes air molecules out of the way. The more air molecules it hits, the more drag it feels. For that reason, drag depends on speed. Also, the larger the frontal area pointing into the flowing air, the greater the drag force. For example, a jet is more streamlined and aerodynamic than a small prop-driven plane because its nose is tapered. To minimize drag for your flyers, you will make them aerodynamic by giving them small pointed fronts to help them slice through the air.

Weight

Weight pulls us down—all of us. Weight is the archenemy of lift for a flying machine. Lift attempts to keep something up and weight pulls it down. Although airplanes (and flyers) must be made of strong materials, those materials must be of the lightest weight possible. The heavier the material, the more lift that's needed to overcome it.

Safety

While building and launching flyers, you have to keep safety in mind. Here are a few rules to make your flying time safe and enjoyable.

1. Always ask for adult permission to build any of the flyers in this book.
2. Never aim a flyer at people, pets, or breakable stuff. Outside is a great place to launch most of these flying machines. You'll have longer flights and less chance

of breaking Mom's glassware. (Most flyers, however, can be flown indoors. Just be cautious when doing so.)

3. Be very careful with scissors. Many of the flying machine materials can be cut with safety scissors, but sometimes sharper points are needed. Have an adult or older sibling help you when you use pointed scissors or a knife.
4. When using a stapler, keep both hands well away from the stapler jaws.

Paper Folding

Paper folding is the key to many good flyers. The best way to fold paper is with your thumb or index finger. Using your thumbnail to completely smooth out creases is also a valuable skill.

In this book, a "hot dog" fold is made lengthwise down the paper. This leaves you with a long, skinny, folded piece of paper just like a hot dog bun. A "hamburger" fold is made across the piece of paper and leaves you with a short, wide, folded piece like a hamburger bun.

Paper Tosses

You will use a variety of paper tosses to get various flyers up, up, and away.

1. Wrist flick: This is the most basic flyer toss. Grab the flyer between your thumb and index finger, then flick your wrist forward away from your body.
2. Frisbee toss: Just like tossing a Frisbee, this method is designed to get the flyer spinning. Place your thumb on top and curl your fingers beneath the flyer. Put your palm toward your belly button. Quickly extend your wrist, and away your flyer will spin.
3. Boomerang toss: Boomerangs are actually thrown overhead. Grab the bottom of the boomerang, then hold it over your throwing shoulder almost perfectly upright. Extend your elbow and let it fly forward. The boomerang toss takes practice to perfect. The Aussie is the perfect flyer to practice with. Boomerang pros have to practice for a long time to master the curved flyer, so be patient.

4. Finger flick: The finger flick is a valuable technique for the Basic Fingerrang and all of its cousins. The flick is done by curling your finger to below the knuckle of your thumb. The more you curl it, the more energy you store in your finger. Using muscles to straighten your finger will cause the Fingerrang to flick forward. Some people use their index finger, while others find more success with their middle finger. Try both to see what works best for you.

2

Rockets

You can use common materials to make fun flying rockets. The rockets in this chapter will start with simple designs and progress toward the more challenging.

Flight School

Rockets fight a constant battle of thrust, weight, lift, and drag. **Thrust** comes from the rocket engine and pushes the rocket up. At the same time, **weight** pulls down on the rocket, and **drag** also acts against the upward motion. Think of it as a giant game of tug-of-war. For a rocket to lift off, thrust has to win the battle with weight and drag. **Lift** is just a tiny part the process and only happens when the rocket is no longer going straight up.

Rocket thrust comes from the rocket's engine. Usually this power comes from burning rocket fuel, but in the flyers you'll build it will come from rubber bands and air pressure. Your family probably wouldn't approve of you burning rocket fuel in the house anyway. But you may want to try building model rockets someday—they do burn rocket fuel.

Rockets are stabilized and steered by the fins on the side and by redirecting the engine nozzles. The fins redirect air just like flaps on a plane. The engine nozzles can be redirected by the use of gimbals, which allow the nozzle to swing in different directions. The gimbals redirect thrust and allow the rocket to launch at the correct angle.

When the rocket gets to space, tiny retroactive rocket engines steer the craft. Retro rockets only blow in one direction, but each faces a different direction. When fired in the right combination using Isaac Newton's Third Law of Motion (for every action, there is an equal and opposite reaction), the rocket will turn. Similar retro rockets allow the rocket to speed up or slow down as needed. There is no drag in space because there is no atmosphere, so the rocket just keeps zipping along at a constant speed until the retro rockets fire. Over 99 percent of the rocket fuel is used up during launch to overcome weight and drag to propel the rocket into space.

Let's stay on Earth and build our own rockets.

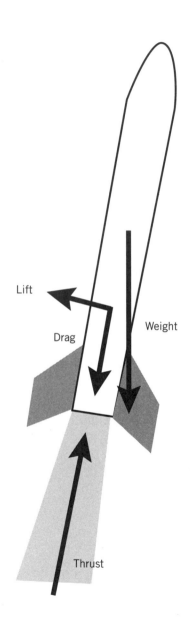

Basic Straw Rocket

A simple rubber band will launch this Basic Straw Rocket high above the treetops.

Flight Gear

Drinking straw
Scissors
Index card (or scrap cardstock)
Stapler
Rubber band
Ruler

Step 1: Using your thumb and index finger, flatten one end of a drinking straw.

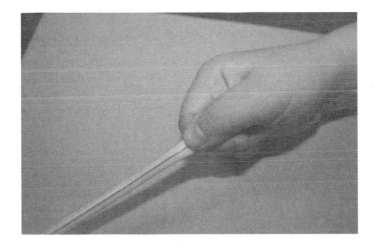

Step 2: Using scissors, cut the flat end of the straw about 1 inch from the tip.

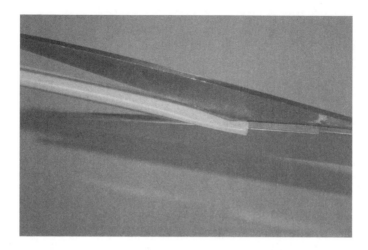

Step 3: Cut two strips, each 1 inch by 3 inches, from an index card to create the rocket's fins. (Note: You can also use magazine insert cards or any scrap cardstock.)

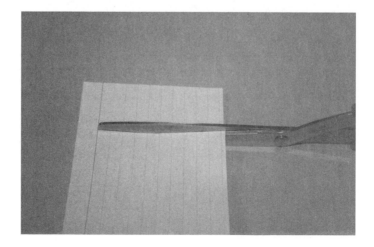

Step 4: Insert the two strips into the slit that you cut in the end of the straw. Staple them securely. These will be the rocket fins. *Don't fold them out yet.*

Step 5: Insert a rubber band about 1 inch into the other end of the straw.

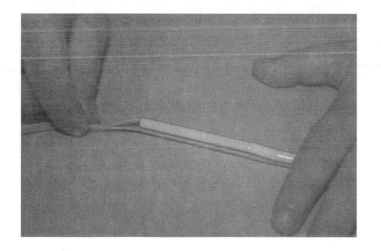

Step 6: Staple across the rubber band end of the straw. Take care to "capture" the rubber band through the two prongs of the staple. Stapling through the rubber band itself weakens the rubber band and leads to shorter flights (and broken rubber bands). If the rubber band breaks, just staple in another one.

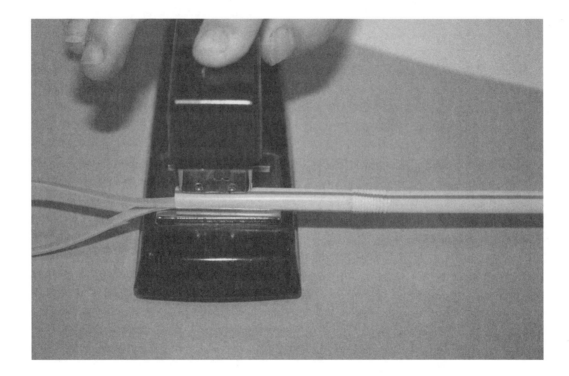

Step 7: Fold out the fins to create an *X*.

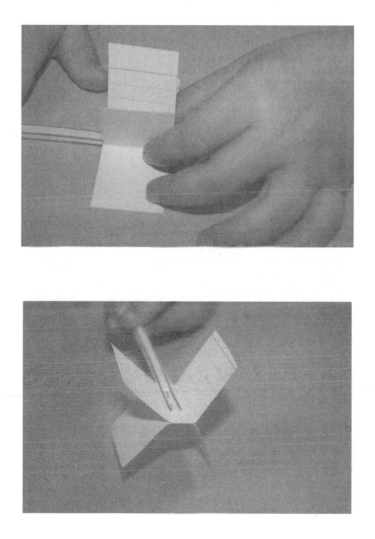

Step 8: Hook the rubber band on the end of the ruler. Hold the fins and pull back. Let go of the fins and watch the rocket blast off. Instead of the ruler, you can also use the Straight-as-an Arrow Launcher (page 164).

Advanced Flight Topics

While flying your Basic Straw Rocket, here are a few experiments you can do: Pull back the rubber band to different lengths and see how that changes the flight path. Try bending the fins to get the rocket to spin as it flies. Launch your rocket at different angles. Which angle gives you the greatest distance? Which angle gives you the greatest time in the air? Challenge a friend to build his or her own rocket and then have a rocket race.

Cruise Missile

Build this super sleek high-flying cruise missile that can fly over your house.

Flight Gear

Three drinking straws
Scissors
Clear tape
Scrap cardstock
Rubber band
Ruler

Step 1: Use the scissors to cut three straws so they are each about 4 inches long. Then cut one of the straws to be ¼ inch shorter.

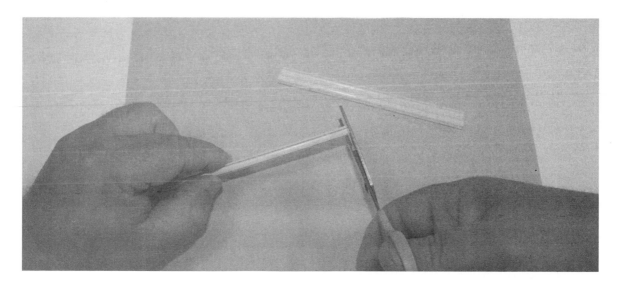

Step 2: Stack the straws in a triangle and even up one end. Wrap a piece of tape around that end. This will be the rear end of the Cruise Missile.

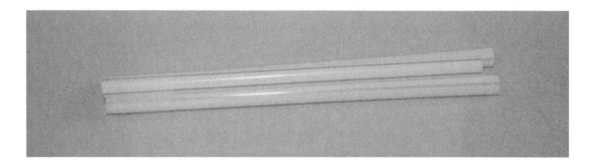

Step 3: Cut a ½-inch-wide strip of scrap cardstock—magazine covers, index cards, file folders, or old greeting cards will all work. Fold the strip exactly in half and press down the crease with your thumbnail. Then, from the fold, measure 1 inch and bend both wings out. The double fold will be the tail and the single thicknesses will be the wings. The wing/tail assembly should look like a *Y*, as shown. Don't worry yet about the wings' length; you will trim them later.

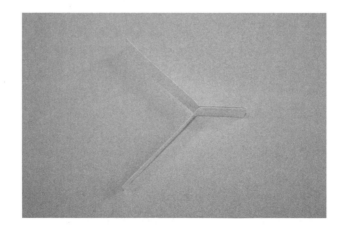

Step 4: Slide the tail (double fold) between the two long straws. The wings should come out between the long and short straws on either side. Slide all the way until you reach the tape strip at the rear.

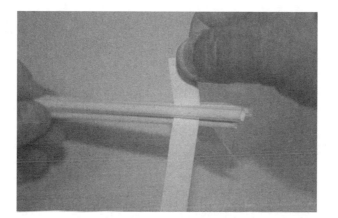

Step 5: Wrap a piece of tape around the straws just in front of the wing/tail assembly to hold it in place. Trim the wings to the desired length. (You might try 1 inch for your first Cruise Missile.) You can make them all the same length, but you don't have to.

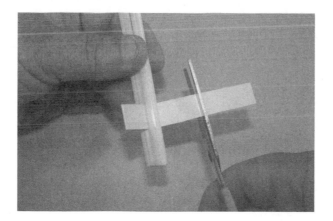

Step 6: Take a piece of tape and hold the sticky side up. Lay a rubber band across the tape so that it sticks. Make sure the rubber band is flat on the tape.

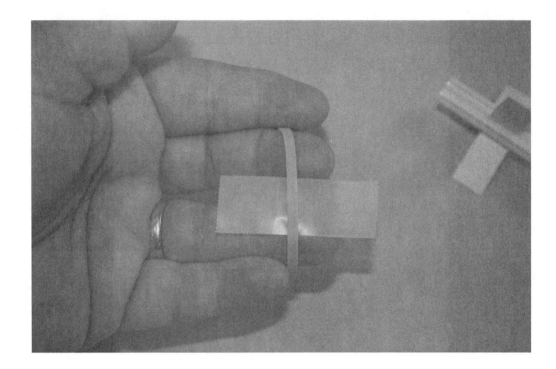

Step 7: Place the rubber band beneath the bottom (short) straw and press up. Wrap the tape ends around the nose of the Cruise Missile.

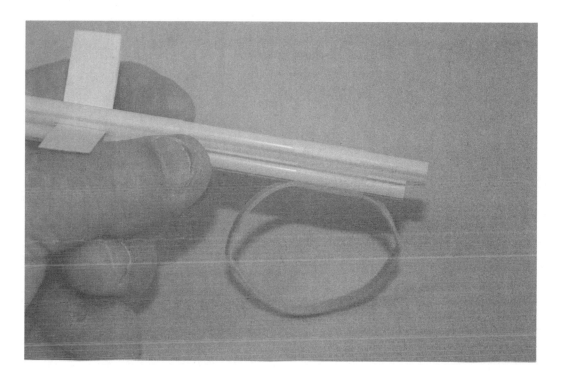

Step 8: Now you are ready to launch your Cruise Missile. Hook the rubber band on the ruler (or the Straight-as-an-Arrow Launcher from page 164). Pull back the rubber band and let the Missile fly. *Remember: Don't aim at friends, pets, or Mom's breakable stuff.*

Advanced Flight Topics

Thrust is key for rockets, so pull harder on the rubber band to make the Missile go farther. You can easily cut and replace the front tape to experiment with different size rubber bands. You can also try full-size straws to see how the flight path changes or build the Cruise Missile with bigger (or smaller) wings and see what happens.

Bottle Rocket

An empty water bottle and a big foot will help this rocket soar 20 to 30 feet.

Flight Gear

Scissors
Sheet of paper
Flexible drinking straw
Clear tape
Masking tape
Duct tape
Empty plastic water bottle
Optional: small weights, such as pebbles or marbles

Step 1: Use the scissors to cut a sheet of paper into fourths. Roll one ¼ sheet around the straw but make sure it is not too tight since the straw will be the launch pad. Wrap a small piece of clear tape around both ends and the middle of your rocket to form a tube.

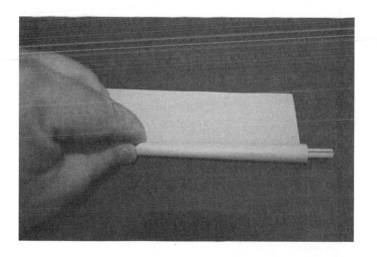

Step 2: Fold one end of the rocket body tube over and secure it with clear tape. This will be the nose of the rocket.

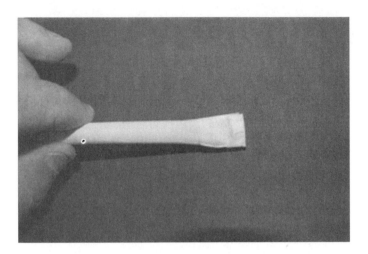

Step 3: Now it's time to make the tail fin. Lay a 3-inch piece of masking tape on the table, sticky side up. Then place the tail of the rocket in the center of the sticky side.

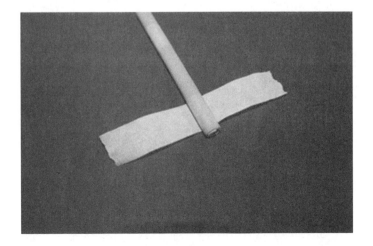

Step 4: Place another 3-inch piece of masking tape over the top of the other one, but put this piece sticky side down. Don't worry if the pieces aren't exactly the same size. You'll trim the fins in the next step.

Step 5: Use the scissors to trim the fins. Cut from the back of the rocket and angle the outside edge of the fins toward the nose as shown. You can add a second set of fins if you want in the same manner—just place the second set above (closer to the nose) and perpendicular to the first set. The Bottle Rocket should look like an *X* from behind if you do that.

Step 6: Now it is time to build the launcher. Bend a flexible straw at a 45-degree angle. Use a large square of duct tape to keep the angle in place. Duct tape is never pretty, but it is very sticky, so it works very well.

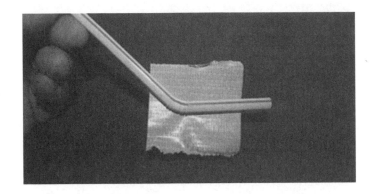

Step 7: Look for a new, eco-friendly style of water bottle made with thinner plastic. It will work the best for your launcher because it's more flexible, but any plastic bottle will work. Set the bottle on a table and let it roll to see which side naturally faces down. Place the short end of the bent straw into the bottle until the duct tape just hits the mouth of the bottle. The long end of the straw should be pointing up into the air. Use a few narrow strips of duct tape to seal the short end of the straw in the mouth of the bottle.

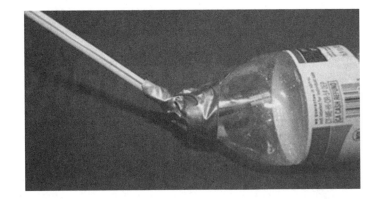

Step 8: Slide the rocket onto the launch pad (the angled straw). If the bottle rolls or tilts the straw launcher toward the ground, you will need to add some weight to the bottom of the bottle. A few pennies and tape should do the trick, but any weight (pebbles, marbles, etc.,) will do. You can skip the weight if your bottle lies flat without a weight.

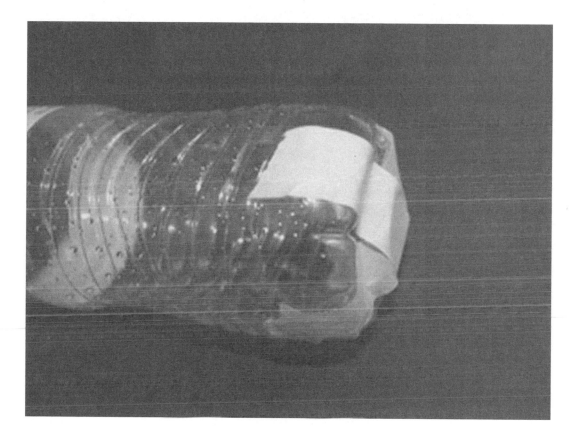

Step 9: Aim the rocket away from people, pets, and breakable stuff. Stomp on the middle of the bottle, but avoid stepping on the end. The end is not as flexible, and if it cracks, you'll have to build another launcher. The harder you stomp, the farther the rocket

will fly, but never use both feet under any circumstances—one foot must always be on the ground! For the next launch, you can usually pop out the flattened water bottle by blowing through the straw.

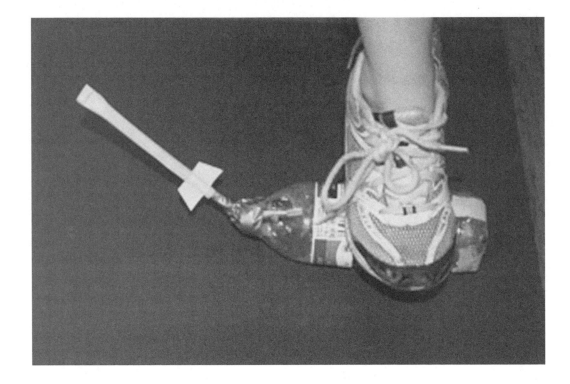

Advanced Flight Topics

Rockets fly farther because of thrust. Your foot supplies the air pressure thrust, so try stomping harder. You might even ask an older brother, sister, or parent to send your rocket into high orbit. As an experiment, use a larger 2-liter bottle for your launcher but be very careful and keep one foot firmly planted on the ground.

Soda Pop Rocket

Launch the Soda Pop Rocket across the backyard with just a hard squeeze.

Flight Gear

2 drinking straws of different diameters
Empty plastic drink bottle
Modeling clay or Play-Doh
Masking tape
Scissors

Step 1: You will make the launcher first. Insert the thinner straw in the mouth of an empty plastic drink bottle. Use a piece of clay or Play-Doh to seal off the mouth of the bottle. Be careful not to get any inside the straw or it will block the airflow. Eco-friendly thin plastic bottles work best for the launcher.

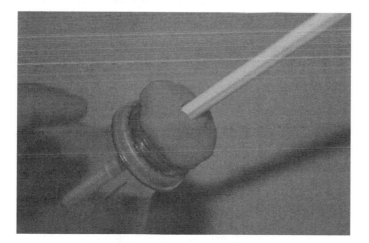

Step 2: Now you will build the rocket. Make the nose first. Fold over the end of the wider straw. Wrap the bent-over end of the straw with masking tape to hold it in place.

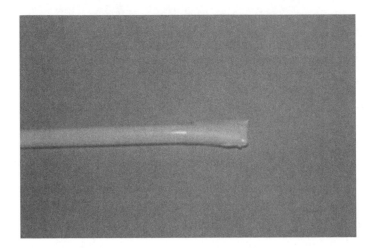

Step 3: To make the tail, lay a piece of masking tape under the rocket straw with the sticky side up. Lay another piece of masking tape over the top of the rocket straw with the sticky side down. Press the two pieces of tape together.

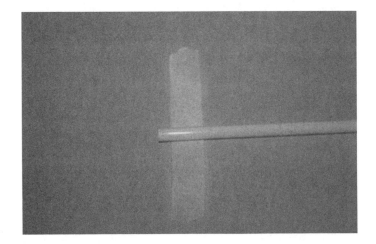

Step 4: Repeat Step 3 to create another set of fins. Place this set directly in front of the first set but perpendicular to it. Use scissors to trim all four tail fins to the desired lengths and shapes.

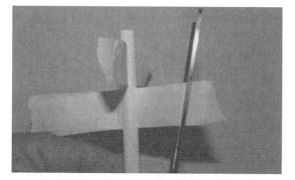

Step 5: Now you are ready to launch your Soda Pop Rocket. Place the rocket straw over the launcher straw. Squeeze the bottle as hard as you can and watch your rocket blast off. You can blow back through the smaller straw to "reload" your launcher and blast off again.

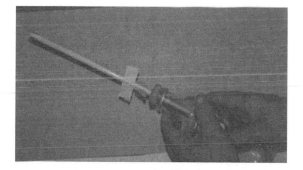

Advanced Flight Topics

Try squeezing harder on the launcher bottle to create more pressure—pressure equals thrust for the Soda Pop Rocket. For another experiment, curve the fins to watch your rocket spin.

Blow Darts

Hit targets across the room with tiny Blow Darts.

Flight Gear

2 drinking straws of different diameters
Scissors
Modeling clay, Play-Doh, or a slice of raw potato

Step 1: Make sure the smaller straw will slide inside the larger straw without getting stuck. (Blow darts work best if the straws are close in size.) Use scissors to cut the smaller straw into four or five tiny straws, each about 2 inches long. Push one end of each straw through the clay or Play-Doh to seal one end. You can also use a slice of raw potato about ¼-inch thick.

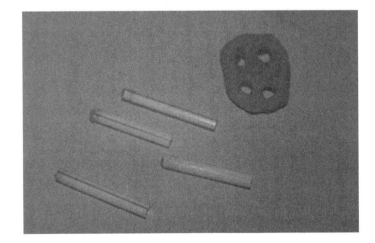

Step 2: Slide one of the Blow Darts into the launcher straw. Slide the blocked end in first. Push it in just far enough to be hidden within the launcher straw.

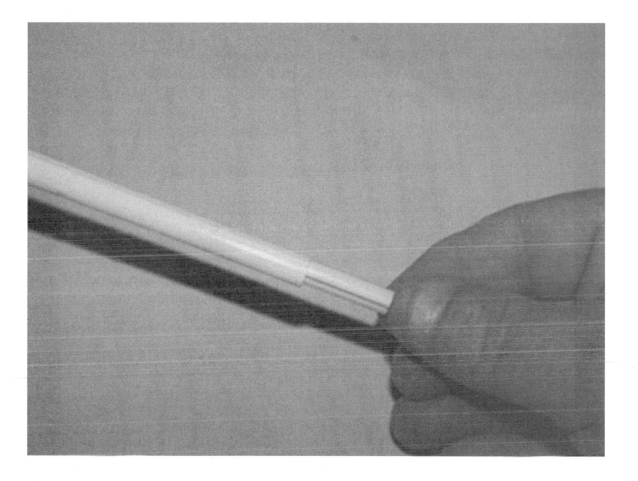

Step 3: Put the end closest to the Blow Dart into your mouth. Close your lips around the launcher straw and blow—*but do not inhale!* A quick exhale works the best. As always, aim away from pets, friends, and breakable stuff.

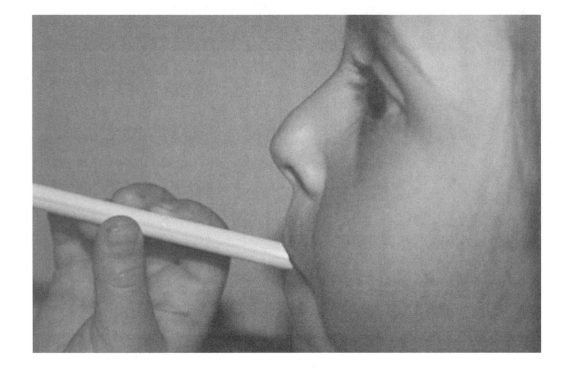

Advanced Flight Topics

Blow darts are used by hunters around the world. Set up a target and see if you can hit the bull's-eye like a hunter.

Whisper Rocket

Turn scrap paper into a rubber band–powered rocket and have fun blasting off.

Flight Gear

Paper clip
One-half sheet of paper
Stapler
Clear tape
Rubber band

Step 1: Bend down the free end of the *inner* loop of a paper clip.

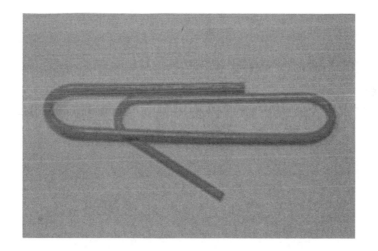

Step 2: Fold the half sheet of paper, hot dog bun style. Place the paper clip between the half-sheet of paper, at the fold. Staple twice through both sides of the hot dog fold, making sure both staples have captured the paper clip.

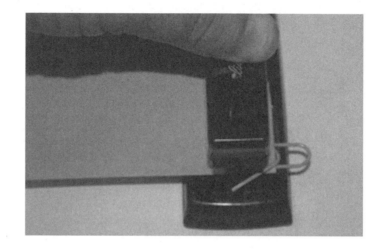

Step 3: Slide the paper clip outward until it hits the staples. Fold the paper down by making a valley fold (a valley fold is done by creasing the paper and folding the sides up so the paper looks like a valley) even with the top of the paper clip. Repeat making folds, accordion-style, until all your paper is used up. The resulting paper should look like a fan that is folded up from the top. Wrap the nose of the rocket securely with tape.

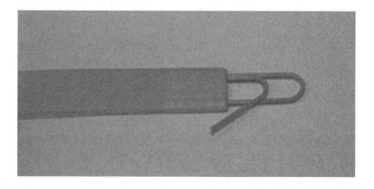

Step 4: Place another piece of tape around the center of the rocket. Spread out the back of the rocket like a fan. Finally, pull the free end of the paper clip down even farther. This will allow the Whisper Rocket to launch freely.

Step 5: Now you are ready to launch. Place a rubber band between your thumb and index finger. Hook the free end of the paper clip on the rubber band. Pinch the middle of the rear wing, pull back, and let the Rocket fly.

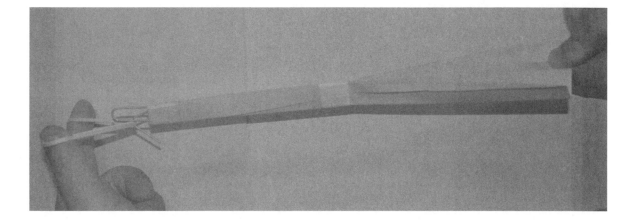

Advanced Flight Topics

Try two, three, and four rubber bands between your fingers for more thrust. You can also try making the Whisper Rocket with different size pieces of paper.

3

Hand-Powered Gliders

Fun flyers that are easy to build, fun to fly, and powered by hand.

Flight School

Flight is possible because of the tug-of-war involving lift, thrust, drag, and weight. But steering a plane takes a little more flight dynamics. Pilots owe it all to a set of moving flaps that redirect the air and allow pilots to control the plane.

Let's start at the back. The tail has a vertical flap called a **rudder**. The rudder allows the plane to turn left and right, just like the rudder on a boat. The two horizontal flaps are called **elevators**. And they allow the plane to go up or down.

The main wing has two sets of flaps. The outermost flaps are called the **ailerons**. These flaps allow one end of the wing to create more lift than the other end. This will bank the plane and allow it to turn right or left. The innermost flaps are just called **flaps**. The flaps allow you to raise or lower the nose of the plane. Flaps are also important because they can create extra drag, which is necessary to slow the plane for landing.

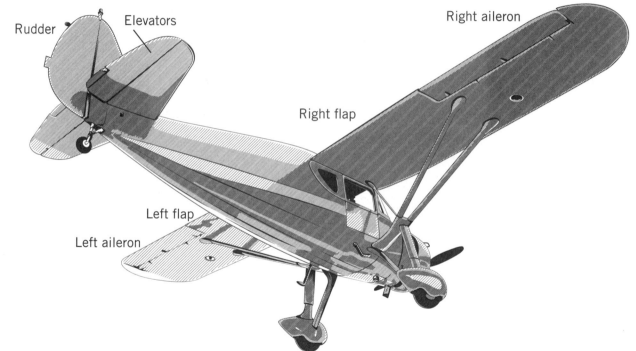

Rudder

Elevators

Right aileron

Right flap

Left flap

Left aileron

Now that we are on the ground, let's build more flyers.

Flying Flounder

Watch the Flying Flounder as it flops like a fish, all the way to the ground.

Flight Gear

Strip of scrap paper
Scissors
Colored pens (to decorate)

Step 1: Cut a long strip of scrap paper, any size. (The strip shown is 2 inches by 8 inches.) This flyer is a perfect use for scrap paper or for cool artwork, like magazine covers, ads, or your report card (just kidding). You can make an entire family of Flying Flounders from different types of scrap paper.

Next, use the scissors to make a very small cut ½ inch from the end of the Flounder. The cut should go exactly halfway across the strip of paper. Make another small cut on the other end of the strip, but on the opposite side as shown.

75 percent actual size

If you're using plain scrap paper, you can use colored pens to decorate both sides of the strip with words or artwork. Loop the paper over on itself and slide the two small cuts you made into each other.

Step 2: Now prepare to launch the world's easiest flyer. Pinch the top of the Flying Flounder between your fingers. Lift it as high as you can and let it drop. Now enjoy the show as it makes crazy flips.

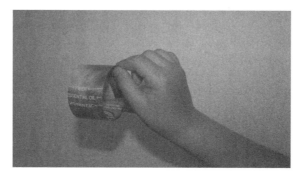

Advanced Flight Topics

Drop it from as high as you can. Second-floor balcony? Perfect. High outside deck? Another great spot! Try to count the number of revolutions as it falls. What about a tiny Flying Flounder? How well does it fly?

Plastic Zipper

Just a flick of your wrist launches the Plastic Zipper on a crazy, curving flight.
Adult supervision required

Flight Gear

Empty plastic drink bottle
Sharp knife
Scissors
Duct tape (or wide masking tape)
Permanent marker (optional)

Step 1: Rinse out a plastic drink bottle. Have an adult helper use a sharp knife to cut through the bottle near the top and near the bottom. You can now use the knife to cut the entire top and bottom off *if you have permission*. (If you cut them all the way off, skip the next step.)

Step 2: Slide the bottom blade of a pair of scissors into one of the knife cuts. Cut around the bottle. Try to keep the cut straight, but you can always even it up later. Once you have cut off both the top and bottom, you will have a plastic tube left over.

Step 3: Wrap a piece of duct tape (or wide masking tape) around one edge of the Plastic Zipper. Leave at least one fourth of the tape hanging over the edge.

Step 4: Fold the remaining tape down *inside* the Plastic Zipper. If you have a permanent marker, draw racing stripes (or other cool artwork) on the side.

Step 5: Now it's time to unleash this flying machine. Grab the Plastic Zipper like you grab a football. The taped edge should point forward, as shown. As you throw it, make sure to let it roll off your fingers so it will spiral. An even easier way to get it to spiral is to throw it underhand or sidearm.

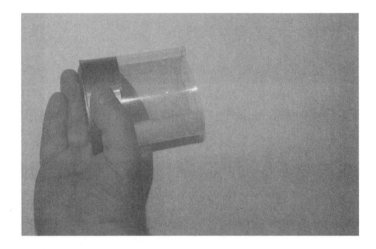

Advanced Flight Topics

The spin and arm angle are the keys to a successful flight. Try an underhand, overhand, and sidearm throw to see which is best for maximum distance. Or try adding more weight to the front tape ring, either extra tape or paper clips, to increase the inertia and make it fly farther.

Paper Plate Flyer

Slightly used paper plates turn into a flyer that will cruise 50 feet with just a flick of your wrist. *Adult supervision required*

Flight Gear

Sharp knife
4 or 5 paper plates
Scissors
White glue
Pens, pencils, or crayons

Step 1: Have an adult use a sharp knife to make a small cut through each of the paper plates. Each small cut should be made right along the edge of the flat bottom, as shown.

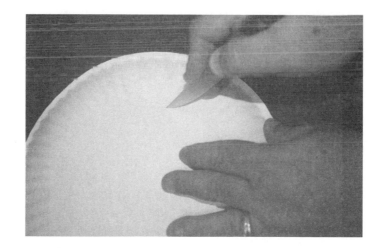

Step 2: Use scissors to cut out each flat bottom of the paper plates. This is easier to do if you cut from the bottom of the plate.

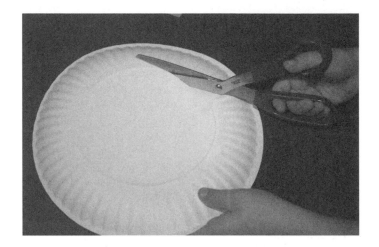

Step 3: Put a bead of glue around the inside top of all but one of the plates.

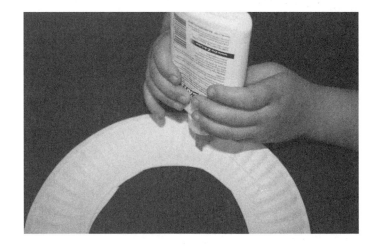

Step 4: Sandwich the glue-covered plates together, place the nonglued plate on top, and press them all together into one big ring.

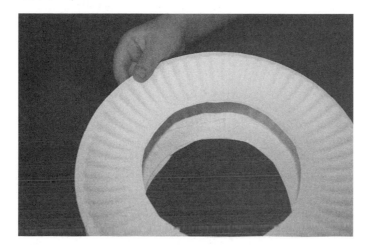

Step 5: Use your fingers to press the plates together. Move around the flyer several times to squish the glue out really well.

Step 6: Use pens, pencils, or crayons to decorate the curved part of the plates. The bottom of the glued plates will be the top of the flyer.

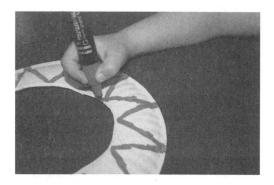

Step 7: Now you are ready to fly. The Paper Plate Flyer works like a Frisbee. Place your thumb on top and wrap your fingers around under the edge. Extending your wrist quickly will cause it to spin and fly. The more spin, the better.

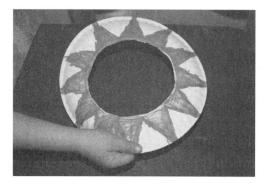

Advanced Flight Topics

Frisbees work because the spinning edge provides lift. Throwing the Paper Plate Flyer at different angles will even allow you to play catch with yourself.

Red Baron

Just two fingers can launch this super-soaring machine over 30 feet.

Flight Gear

2 strips of paper
Scissors
Clear tape
1 drinking straw

Step 1: You need two strips of paper that are slightly wider than your tape. Cut one about 4 inches long and the other about 6 inches long, but they don't have to be exactly those sizes. Wrap the two strips into circles and secure with a small piece of tape.

Step 2: Use a small piece of tape to secure the *inside* of the round loop to the straw. Repeat for the other loop at the rear of the Red Baron. Press the tape down and try

not to crease the loops. Keep the loops in line and as parallel as possible. If they aren't parallel, the Red Baron will curve in flight.

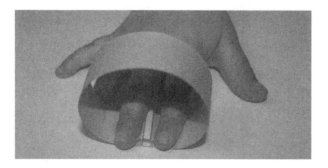

Step 3: You are now ready to launch the Red Baron. With your fingertip and thumb tip, lightly grasp the Red Baron between the loops. Lightly flick your wrist forward and watch the Red Baron glide. An easy toss works better with this flying machine. This flyer works really well launched from a balcony or deck.

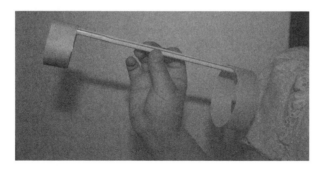

Advanced Flight Topics

Try flying the Red Baron with the loops up or with the big loop in front. Experiment with different sized loops, but be careful. If the back loop gets too big, it will hit your throwing hand every time. Have fun!

Round Square Flyer

A square piece of paper makes a crazy round flyer, capable of flying across any room.

Flight Gear

Square piece of paper (or a paper napkin)
Clear tape

Step 1: Fold the square piece of paper from corner to corner diagonally. Press down the crease with your thumbnail.

Step 2: Make a ¼-inch fold along the long diagonal edge and press down the fold with your thumbnail. Repeat two more times along the same long diagonal.

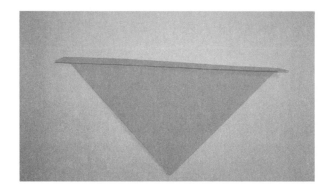

Step 3: Pick up the two long points and bend them into a circle. One of the long points can tuck inside the other one.

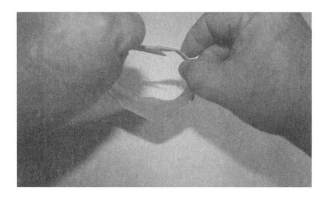

Step 4: Wrap a small piece of tape around the two strip points to hold them together. Now make a better circle out of the multilayered front. Place your thumb inside the front and your fingers outside. Squeeze them together and rotate the round part of

the Round Square Flyer. This will soften the folded paper rim and get rid of any other paper folds that are present.

Step 5: Now you are ready to fly. Grasp the back point of the Round Square Flyer. Launch it from as high as possible. Give it a slight push forward as you launch it.

Advanced Flight Topics

Another challenging way to throw the Square Round Flyer is overhead, like a football. The spin will help it sail, but it takes practice to get good. Throwing it underhand (and spinning it) will also work, just like with the Plastic Zipper.

Three-Penny Flyer

The Three-Penny Flyer will fly across the yard with a simple toss.

Flight Gear

Scissors
3 flexible drinking straws
Piece of paper
Pencil
Three pennies
Clear tape
White glue (optional)

Step 1: Use the scissors to make a small cut in the flex end of each straw. This will allow you to insert the straws into one another.

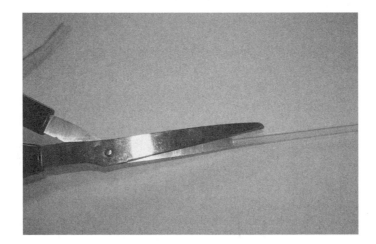

Step 2: Make a triangle by inserting the straws into each other and bending the flexes as needed.

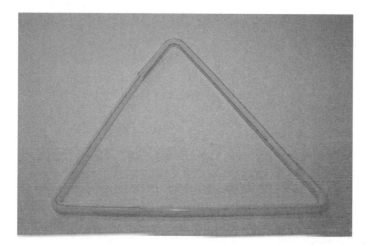

Step 3: Cut three strips of paper, each about 2 inches wide. Cut across the short side of the sheet to save paper.

Step 4: Lay the strips of paper under one side of the triangle. Line up one edge of the paper with the middle of the triangle corner.

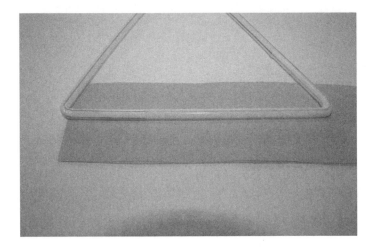

Step 5: Using a pencil, trace the inside edges of the straw triangle to get the angle correct on the paper. Now cut the ends at the desired angles. Repeat for the other two edges.

Step 6: Place one cut paper piece under one triangle edge and place a penny at each end, inside the triangle.

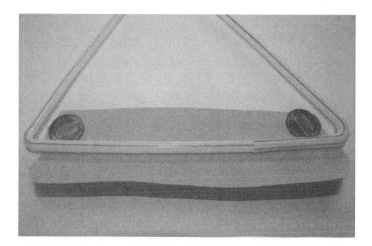

Step 7: Repeat for each side. Use a small piece of tape to hold the pennies in place.

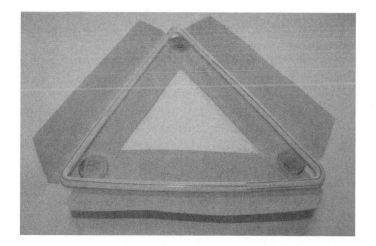

Step 8: Fold the paper over each side. You can glue the inside of each and secure with tape if desired, but tape alone will also work. A small piece of tape in the center will hold the folded paper together for the next step.

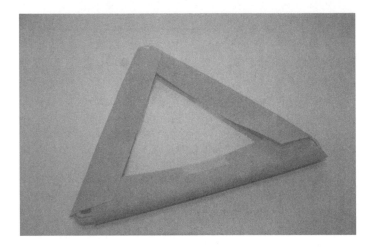

Step 9: Use tape to secure the entire inside of the triangle together. It works best to press the tape on the inside of the paper, leaving half loose. Pick up the flyer, flip it over, and press the tape onto the other side.

Step 10: You are ready to fly. Throw the Three-Penny Flyer like you are throwing a Frisbee.

Advanced Flight Topic

This flyer works best outside since it will cover long distances. Challenge a friend to see who can throw the greatest distance with the Three-Penny Flyer.

Phonebook Flipper

You provide the power to steer this wacky flipping machine anywhere you want it to go.

Flight Gear

Scissors
Phonebook page (or piece of tissue paper)
Ruler
Piece of cardboard

Step 1: Use the scissors to cut a 2-inch by 7-inch piece of phonebook paper. The size can vary as long as the dimensions are approximately the same. Fold up ½ inch of each end at a right angle.

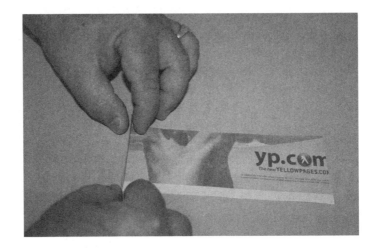

Step 2: Fold up a ¼-inch strip between the two end folds, along one long edge. It helps to fold down the ends while you do this step. Press the crease down with your fingers but stop about ½ inch away from the folded-up ends.

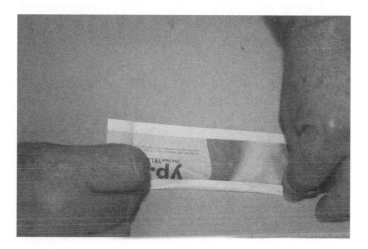

Step 3: Turn the flipper over and repeat for the bottom. You should end up with one long edge flipped down and one long edge flipped up. This will help the Phonebook Flipper flip as it falls.

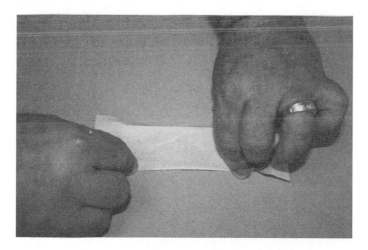

Step 4: Bend the ends back up. Use your fingers to smooth the front and back edge folds to the end folds. Any kinks in the paper will affect the aerodynamics of your Flipper.

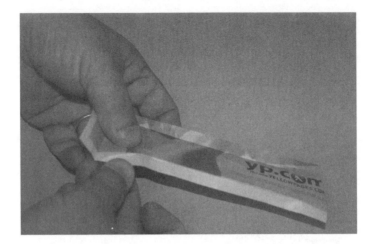

Step 5: To launch, pinch the center of the Phonebook Flipper in the middle of the flat part. The front edge should be flipped down and the back edge flipped up.

Step 6: For best results, you need to launch indoors away from air conditioning vents, since the Phonebook Flipper is so light. With your free hand, hold the cardboard behind and slightly lower than the Phonebook Flipper, as shown. To launch, simply let go of the flipper. Quickly move your launching hand back to the cardboard and follow the Phonebook Flipper to create lift over the cardboard. By angling the cardboard, air that hits the cardboard will be forced up the front of the cardboard. This will make a "wave" of air that creates lift. It will take lots of practice to get this right. If the flipper turns to one side too much, bend up the end on the side that it is turning to.

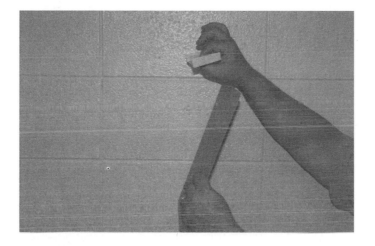

Advanced Flight Topics

Mastering walk-behind gliders is challenging and may take hours of practice. Vary the angle of the cardboard. You can also practice turning the Phonebook Flipper by slightly turning the cardboard. Remember, it takes lots of practice to get good at this, and you will eventually be able to steer the Phonebook Flipper around your house or school.

For more information on walk-behind hang gliders, visit Slater Harrison's website, www.sciencetoymaker.org. It has wonderful videos on how to create even more walk-behind hand gliders. They are fun to fly once you have mastered the skills needed. It takes most of my students several classes to master these crazy, fun flyers. You can master them too with patience and practice.

4

Rubber Band-Powered Gliders

Take airplanes to new heights with the power of rubber bands. Lift, drag, and the Bernoulli principle are all at work to make these gliders fly. Most are tried-and-true paper airplane designs with a few new wrinkles. But rubber band power takes the fun to a new level. You'll start with the all-time favorite, the Classic Dart, try a few new styles, and progress to one of the world's fastest paper airplanes.

Flight School

Like all specialists, pilots have their own lingo. Soccer players use lingo such as *corner kicks*, *offsides*, and *cards* that have certain meanings to other soccer players. Pilots use lingo such as *pitch*, *roll*, *yaw*, and *twelve o'clock*, which mean something to other pilots.

Pilots use yaw, pitch, and roll to describe the motion of their plane. And all three are controlled by the flaps you read about earlier. **Yaw** describes the left/right motion of the plane, which is controlled by the rudder on the tail. **Pitch** describes the nose-up or nose-down position and is controlled by the elevators. **Roll** describes the dipping of one wing, which also helps turn the plane.

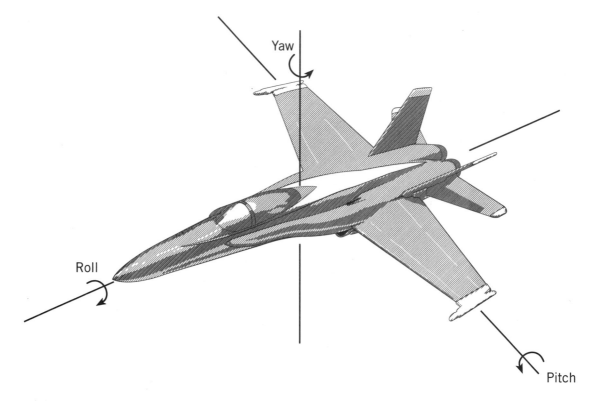

Twelve o'clock may mean lunchtime to you, but it has another meaning for pilots. Imagine you are sitting in the middle of a clock face. Twelve o'clock is directly in front of you. Three o'clock is directly to your right. Six o'clock is behind you, and so on. Using this clock analogy, a pilot can describe the location of other planes in the air.

But now let's get back to building flyers.

Classic Dart

A rubber band amps up the fun of this classic design.

Flight Gear

Sheet of paper
Rubber band
Stapler
Ruler

Step 1: Fold one sheet of paper down the middle, hot dog style.

Step 2: Open the sheet and fold down both corners at a 45-degree angle until they meet the initial fold line.

Step 3: Fold down both top edges again until they meet the center fold line, as shown.

Step 4: Close the center fold by folding the wings up together. Then fold each wing down parallel to the central fold line.

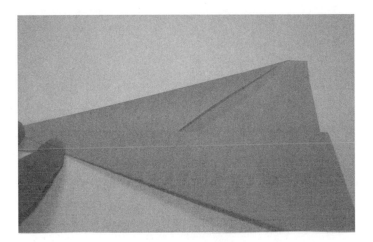

Step 5: After both wings are folded down, use your fingers to press along the entire length of the fold.

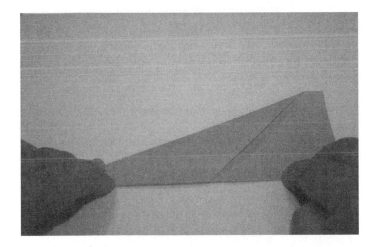

Step 6: Open the plane up. Lay the rubber band inside the nose of the plane.

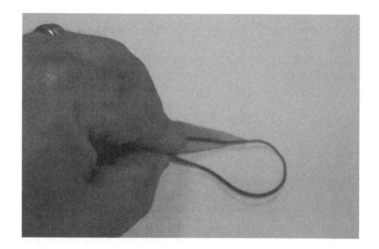

Step 7: Fold the central body of the plane back together. Use the stapler to staple across the nose of the plane. Take care to "capture" the rubber band. Try not to staple through the rubber band itself, since that will make the band weaker, but try to punch the staple through the center of the loop. (If you want, try adding a paper clip to the nose for straighter and longer flights, though the Classic Dart will fly without it.)

Step 8: Hook the rubber band over the end of a ruler or on the notch of the Straight-as-an-Arrow Launcher (page 164). Aim the Classic Dart away from people, animals, or breakable stuff. Pull back and let it fly.

Advanced Flight Topics

Try a few experiments as you launch your Classic Dart. Speed is the fun here, so try pulling back the rubber band to different lengths. Launch the Classic Dart using larger rubber bands, or even try several rubber bands side by side. Try launching at different angles. Or on a windy day, go outside and add a little wind power as you launch.

Flat Flyer

You can make this Flat Flyer soar and twist with just a tug of a rubber band.

Flight Gear

Paper clip
Duct tape (or masking tape)
Piece of paper
Craft stick
Pistol Grip Launcher (or rubber band)

Step 1: Elongate a paper clip by bending out the smaller loop from the larger loop.

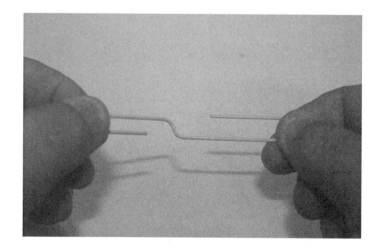

Step 2: Bend the smaller loop back and up so it is at a right angle to the big loop, as shown.

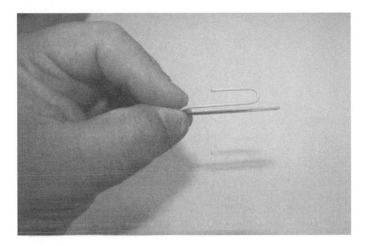

Step 3: Wrap a small strip of duct tape around the large loop. (Masking tape will also work.) The small loop should point up when you're done.

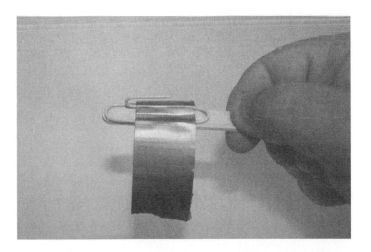

Step 4: Fold a 1-inch strip along the longest side of a sheet of paper.

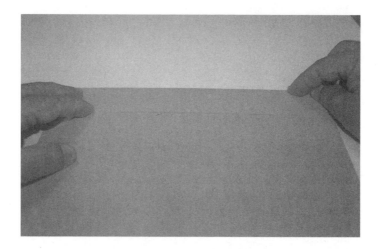

Step 5: Fold the 1-inch strip in half on itself, then flatten it out with your fingertips. This will be the front of your Flat Flyer.

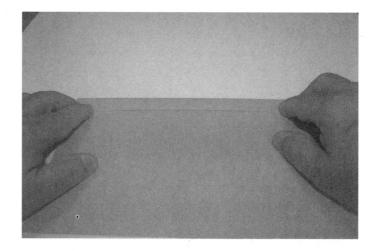

Step 6: Fold in approximately 2 inches of each front corner at a 45-degree angle.

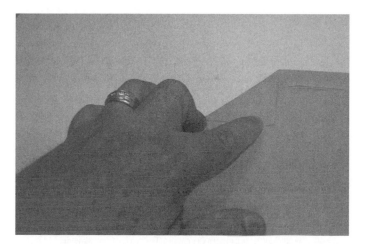

Step 7: Fold both wings up, even with the corner fold you made in the previous step.

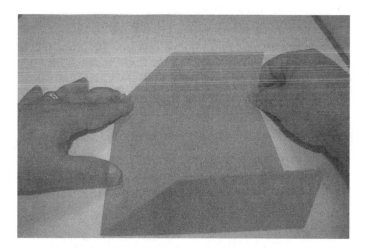

Step 8: Fold each wing inward. Now line the top edge of each wing with the outside of the flat bottom piece. (Refer to Step 9 to see the completed folds.) Use your fingertips to smooth out the folds.

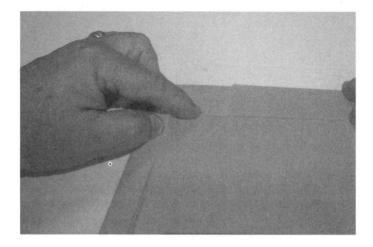

Step 9: Now tape the craft stick and clip to the middle bottom of the Flat Flyer. Make sure the paper clip is at the front and the open loop is correctly placed. It is okay if the craft stick extends past the flat bottom.

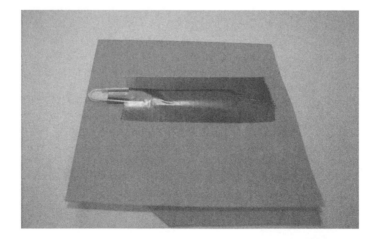

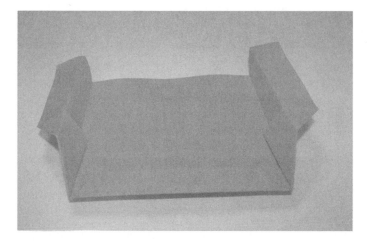

Step 10: Now hook the paper clip loop onto the Pistol Grip Launcher (page 166) and let it fly. You can also use a rubber band between your thumb and index finger if you haven't built the launcher yet.

Advanced Flight Topics

Build another Flat Flyer, but slide the craft stick up so that it sticks out the front. Also, you can cut ailerons (small flaps) in the back of the wings. Bend them up and watch what happens. Bend them down and try it again.

Mini-Delta Flyer

Launch an old greeting card over 50 feet when you make the Mini-Delta Flyer.

Flight Gear

Scissors
Drinking straw
Rubber band
Paper clip
Stapler
Old greeting card
Ruler

Step 1: Use the scissors to cut a drinking straw about two-thirds of the way down, so you are left with a piece about 6 inches long. Cut off the flexible part if it is a flex straw.

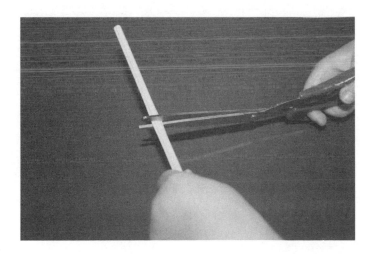

Step 2: Slide a rubber band into a paper clip and pull it to the single-looped end of the clip.

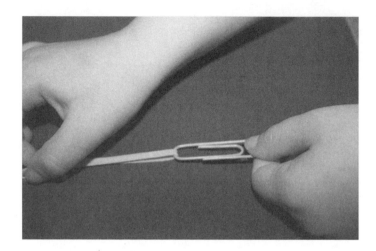

Step 3: Slide the smaller loop of the paper clip into the straw.

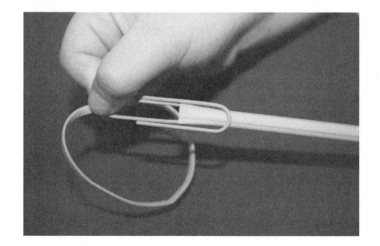

Step 4: Staple through the straw and paper clip. Make sure that you "capture" both loops of the paper clip.

Step 5: Cut an old greeting card in half. Keep the other half for a future flyer.

Step 6: Fold the card piece in half, hot dog style. Use your fingers to press down the crease.

Step 7: With the folded edge of the card near the straw, make a mark slightly shorter than the straw. About ½ inch on both ends is fine.

Step 8: Using your mark as a guide, draw a triangle up from the folded edge. Also, draw a ½-inch line about ½ inch from the rear edge of the wing, as shown.

Step 9: Cut out the delta wing shape. Don't forget to cut the ½-inch slot near the rear edge.

Step 10: The paper clip will be the nose of the Mini-Delta Flyer. Slide the wing onto the straw and under the paper clip in the front. Guide the back end of the straw through the ½-inch slot you cut earlier.

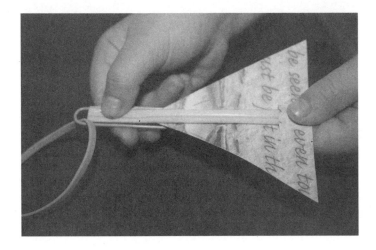

Step 11: Pull the tail of the straw past the wing so your fingers have something to grab during launches.

Step 12: Fold up the outside corners of each wing for additional stability.

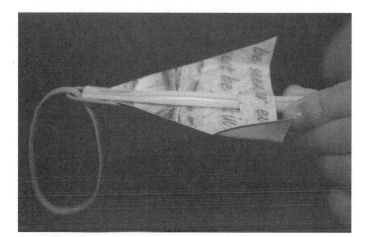

Step 13: Hook the rubber band over the end of a ruler. Aim the Mini-Delta Flyer away from people, animals, or breakable objects. Pull back and let it fly. You can also use the Straight-as-an-Arrow Launcher (page 164) if you already made it.

Advanced Flight Topics

As with any rubber band–powered glider, force matters. You add more launching force by increasing the stretch of the rubber band. The clip allows you to pull harder with this launcher. Also, try different angles for more fun. Or try bending down the wingtips and see if that affects the flight.

F-16

Launch this fast little glider and challenge a friend to a flyer race.

Flight Gear

Scissors
Old greeting card
Pencil
Stapler
Clear Tape
Rubber band

Step 1: Use the scissors to cut an old greeting card into two pieces along the fold. Put aside one half to make another flyer. Fold the card front so that the printed side is on the inside of the fold. This will form the top of the wings on the finished F-16.

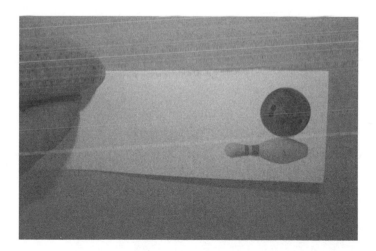

Step 2: Fold each side down about ½ inch. The end of the flyer will look like an *M*. Use your thumbnail to press down the creases.

Step 3: Use a pencil to darken one of the creases on the underside (unprinted side) of the flyer.

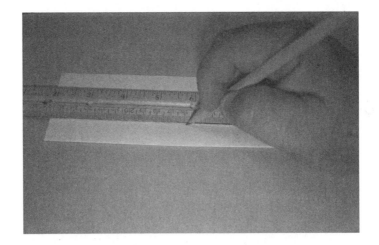

Step 4: Using a pencil, draw in wings and a tail, as shown. An F-16 has front angled wings, but the back of the wing is perpendicular to the body of the plane. Since you are using a pencil, you can erase it and redraw it until you get the shape you want.

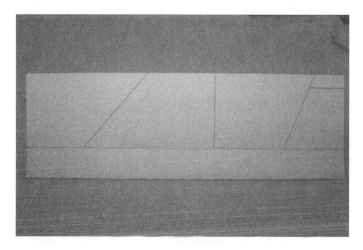

Step 5: Cut the front of the wing down to the body, but do not cut off the front of the wing. Cut between the wing and the tail. This part can be removed from the body, but don't throw it out, since this piece will be used for the vertical tail. Staple under the front wing at both ends and just in front of the tail.

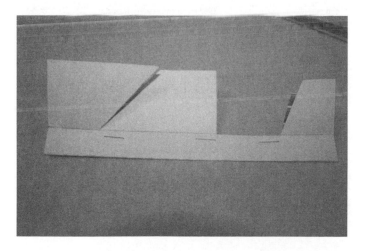

Step 6: Use the piece you removed in Step 5 to make a vertical tail. You probably want to make it shorter, but the angle is already cut for the tail section. Slide the vertical tail in and secure it with a little piece of tape around the back end of the flyer. You can staple through the body beneath the tail if your stapler is strong enough. Either way will work.

Step 7: Fold down the piece in front of the wing and use your thumbnail to press down the crease.

Step 8: Fold the wing front back up, even with the bottom of the body.

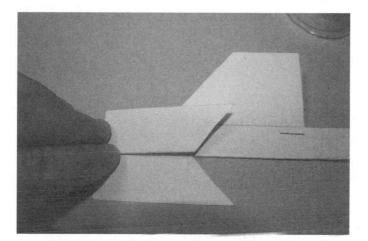

Step 9: Fold the remaining wing front piece back down. Wrap a piece of tape all the way around the nose to secure these folds. You may want to use two pieces of tape for strength. Don't worry if you use too much tape, since it will just add desired nose weight.

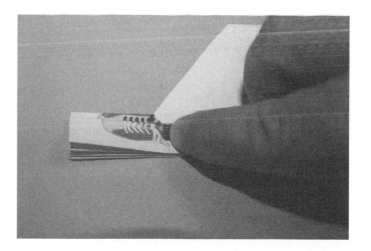

Step 10: Cut a notch on the bottom of the body for a rubber band. Alternatively, you can use a paper clip and rubber band just like you did in the Mini-Delta Flyer and secure the clip with tape. Now you are ready to fly.

Step 11: Place the rubber band over the tip of your thumb and forefinger. Hook the notch on the F-16, pull back, and let it fly. Be careful and aim away from things you could hurt. This flyer is also perfect for the great outdoors.

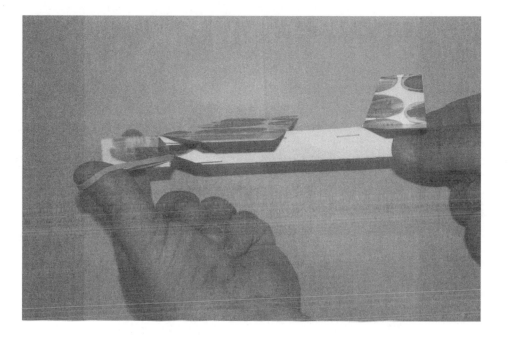

Advanced Flight Topics

You can cut a small flap on the rear of the tail sections. Try folding these flaps in different directions and see which way your F-16 curves. The vertical flap is called a rudder and the horizontal flaps are called elevators.

Falcon Frenzy

Launch this fabulous bird of prey with a mere pull of a rubber band.

Flight Gear

Drinking straw
Scissors
Rubber band
Paper clip
Stapler
Magazine cover (or any heavy paper)
Ruler

Step 1: If you are using a flexible drinking straw, use the scissors to cut off the short flexible end. If you are using a regular drinking straw, you can use the entire straw.

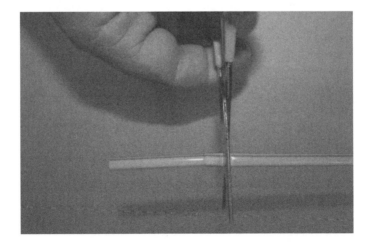

Step 2: Use the scissors to split the entire length of the straw. Once the straw starts to split, you might be able to just slide the scissors down the straw to cut it.

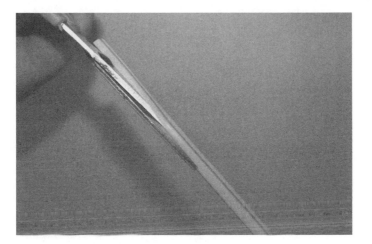

Step 3: Hook a rubber band inside a paper clip. Lay the smallest loop of the paper clip inside one end of the split straw.

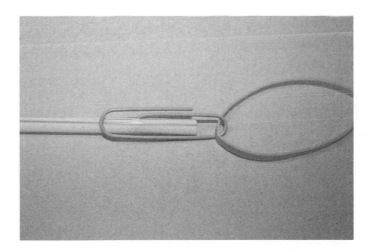

Step 4: Staple through both sides of the straw making sure you "capture" the clip.

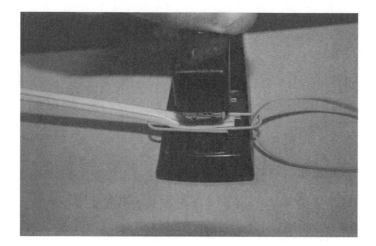

Step 5: Fold the magazine cover hot dog style with the desired wing picture to the *inside* of the fold. Cut out two wings. Make one larger main wing and one smaller tail wing.

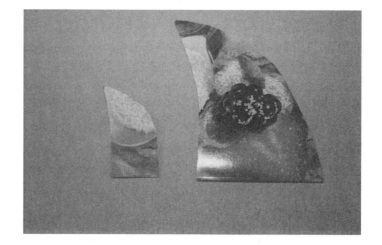

Step 6: Use the stapler to secure both sets of wings to the straw body. You will need two staples for the front wing and one for the rear wing. Make sure you staple through the wing and both sides of the split straw.

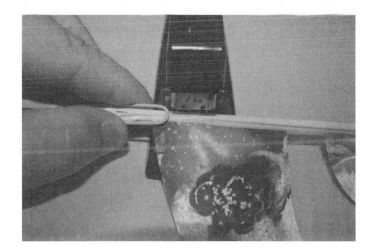

Step 7: Fold down both of the wings and press the crease with your fingertips.

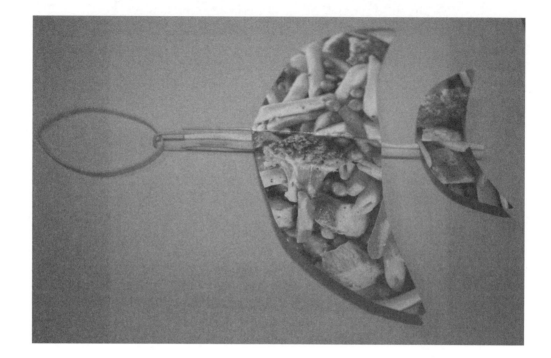

Step 8: Now you are ready to launch. Hook the rubber band on the end of a ruler (or the Straight-as-an-Arrow Launcher on page 164). Pull the tail back and let the Falcon Frenzy soar.

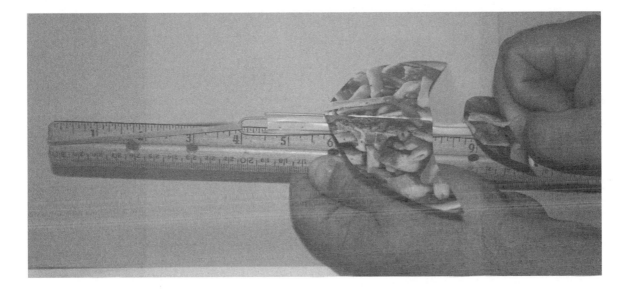

Advanced Flight Topics

Try curving the wings differently to control the flyer's flight. Or bend up the wingtips to see how that changes the flight.

Streak

Send the fastest plane ever on a breathtaking ride.

Flight Gear

Scissors
Paper
Rubber band
Stapler
Ruler

The following are the instructions to make a single Streak. Repeat when you are done to make an air force of four Streaks.

Step 1: Use the scissors to cut the paper into four equal rectangles. Fold one corner all the way over the remaining paper until it reaches the other side. Press down the crease.

Step 2: Now fold the top down until the edges line up. Press down the crease with your finger.

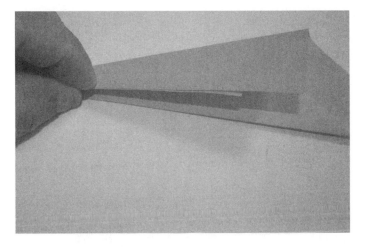

Step 3: Use scissors to cut off just the tip of the Streak. This allows the rubber band to fit through the nose better.

Step 4: Open the crease slightly and place a rubber band inside along the bottom valley fold. Staple the two sides of the Streak above the rubber band. The rubber band will now be captured by the staple.

Step 5: Make an additional fold lengthwise on the Streak. This narrows the front profile and makes it more aerodynamic.

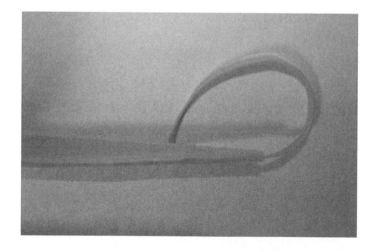

Step 6: You might want to go outside for this speed flyer. Hook the rubber band on the ruler (or use the Straight-as-an-Arrow Launcher on page 164). As always, aim away from people, pets, or breakable stuff. Pull the band back and let the Streak fly.

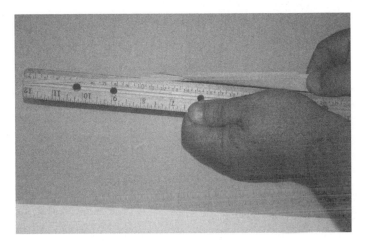

Advanced Flight Topics

Thrust is key for the Streak, so try pulling back harder for a longer flight. You can also try making the Streak with different size rubber bands for maximum speed. Go outside, set up a target, and practice until you are perfect.

Foam Plate Shuttle

Blast off with the high-flying Foam Plate Shuttle.

Flight Gear

Scissors
Foam plate or tray
Ruler
Felt-tip markers
Clear tape
Paper clip
Pistol Grip Launcher

Step 1: Use the scissors to trim off all the raised edges from a foam plate or tray. You should be left with the flat part only. Make one edge of the plate straight to help with Step 2. For safety purposes, never use a foam meat tray that actually contained meat. Foam trays that contained vegetables are fine.

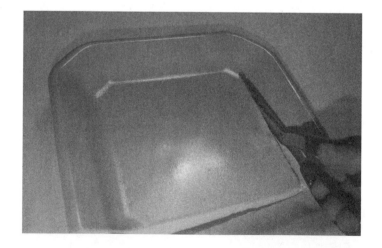

Step 2: Using the photo below as a rough guide, draw a shuttle about half the height of the plate with the rear on the flat edge of the plate. Draw a triangular set of wings using a ruler on the top half of the plate. Use the straight edge as the back of the wing. Draw a slot for the wing in the body of the shuttle. The slot should be as long as the height of the triangle minus 1 inch. Draw a 1-inch slot in the middle of the front of the wing. You want the fit to be tight, so be careful not to make the slot too wide. You can always make it wider as you assemble it, but you can't make it narrower.

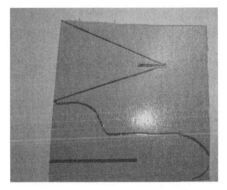

Step 3: Cut out all of the pieces. For the slots, you may have to make two cuts as close as possible depending on the thickness of your foam plate. Now is the perfect time to decorate your shuttle with markers before you put it together.

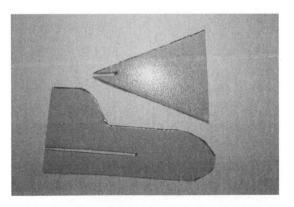

Step 4: Slide the wing into the slot in the body. Make sure to push the wing all the way forward so the front wing slot can lock the wings in place.

Step 5: Place two small pieces of tape underneath each wing to secure it to the body. This tape adds strength to the shuttle.

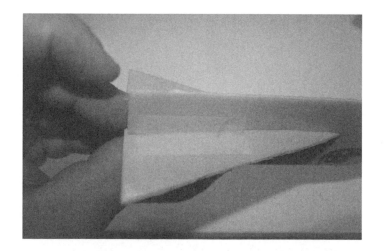

Step 6: Slide a paper clip onto the nose for added weight. Cut a notch under the paper clip to help with launching the shuttle.

Step 7: Hook the rubber band from the Pistol Grip Launcher (page 166) into the notch underneath the Foam Plate Shuttle. Pull back the rubber band by holding the bottom of the body and let the Shuttle fly. You can also fly it without the launcher if you stretch a rubber band between your thumb and forefinger. Hook the notch on the rubber band and let it soar.

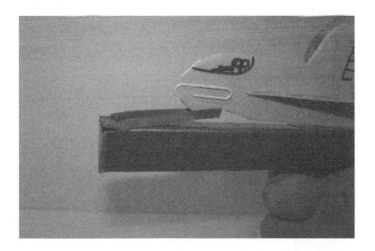

Advanced Flight Topics

As with all rubber band–launched gliders, rubber band stretch is the key. Try different size rubber bands. You can also cut elevator flaps on the rear of the wing. Make two small cuts (½ inch or less) on each side of the tail along the rear wing. Fold up the piece between the cuts and see what happens. Now fold both of them down and watch the flight path. Then try one up and one down. These flaps are one of the ways in which pilots control full-size airplanes. The rudder also controls flight. You can test it by repeating the two cuts on the vertical tail. Bend them right or left to see what happens.

Bat-Wing Flyer

Launch this high flyer and let it dart about like a real-life bat.

Flight Gear

Sheet of copy paper
Ruler
Pencil
Stapler
Rubber band
Clear tape
Scissors
Ruler

Step 1: Fold the piece of paper hamburger style and smooth the crease with your finger. Open the paper back up. Use the ruler to find the exact middle of one half of the paper and make a pencil mark on the long side.

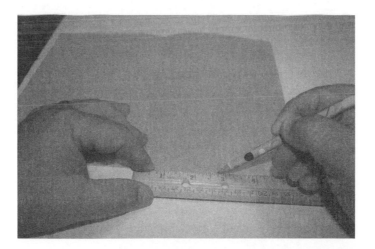

Step 2: Fold the corner down at the pencil mark you just made. Repeat for the other side.

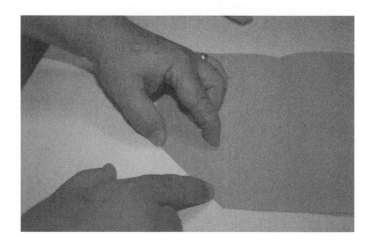

Step 3: Fold the corner again. The edge should now line up with the center hamburger fold. Repeat for the other edge. Press down both wing edges with your fingers.

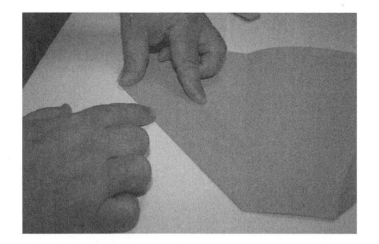

Step 4: Fold the nose back. The tip of the nose should just meet the point where the rear of the wings meets the center hamburger fold.

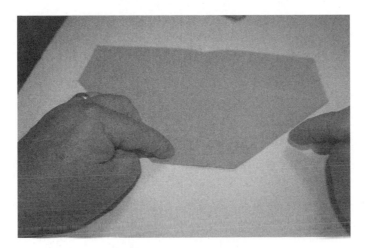

Step 5: Staple a rubber band in the middle of the nose piece. The staple must be directly in the center of the hamburger fold.

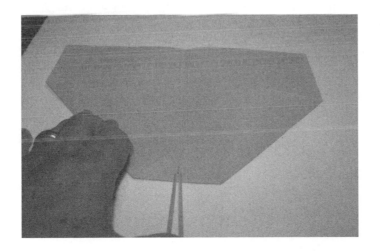

Step 6: You are now going to fold the wings again. Fold each leading edge until it just hits the back of the previous wing fold. Do *not* press down the crease. You want a curved front to the wing to create an airfoil.

Step 7: Tape the wing in place. The easiest way to do this is shown. Use a piece of tape about the length of the entire wing and attach the tape to the bottom edge of the wing with the sticky side up. Half of the tape should be exposed all the length of the wing. Using a thumb and fingers on both ends, curl the wing over and press down the tape. Try not to kink the paper as you do this. (This step to create the airfoil takes

practice and may need to be done several times to get it perfect. Once you master the skill, it is easy to show others.) Repeat for the other wing.

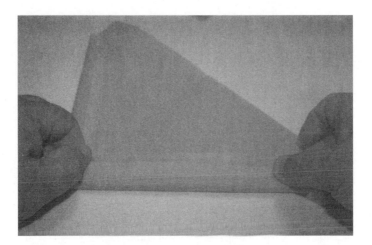

Step 8: Crease the bottom of the center hamburger fold from underneath. You want to crease it almost all the way to the nose. While holding the center bottom fold, use your other hand to curve the wings down. The final Bat-Wing Flyer should look like a slightly curved bat wing when viewed from behind.

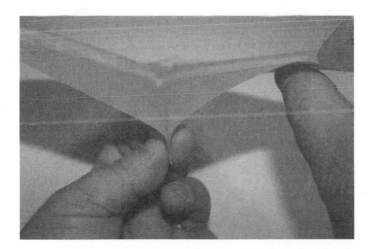

Step 9: Fold the wings together and use the scissors to trim off some of the excess between the wings. There's no need to measure; just make sure you leave some wing area.

Step 10: Time to launch. The Bat-Wing Flyer works best outdoors. It also flies really well on windy days. Hook the rubber band on the ruler or the Straight-as-an-Arrow Launcher (page 164). Aim up in the air and let the Bat-Wing take flight.

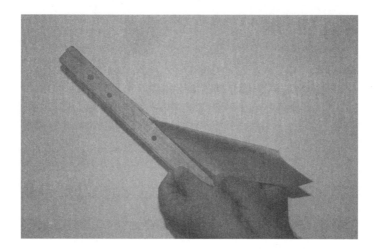

Advanced Flight Topics

Experiment with different launch angles. Then try launching at various angles to the wind. The wind can create crazy flight paths.

5

Helicopters

Spinning blades create fun, free flyers for hours of fun. Helicopter science is the focus of this chapter's flight school. But the real fun comes from flying these crazy, spinning machines.

Flight School

Helicopters create lift by pushing an airfoil (or several) through the air. Thank you, Mr. Bernoulli, for giving us all a lift. The Bernoulli principle allows helicopters to lift straight up, but flying around is bit more complicated. Helicopter pilots' feet and hands are constantly in motion to keep the helicopter flying.

Planes can fly up, down, right, and left, but they must always be moving forward. Helicopters can hover in place, climb straight up, and even fly backward, all because of a few sets of crazy blades. A helicopter needs at least two sets of blades. The **main rotor** on top is the large set of wings that are easiest to see on a helicopter. They generate lift and help steer. The **tail rotor** is the small set of blades on the rear of the helicopter. The tail rotor creates sideways "lift"—though it doesn't make the helicopter go up. Instead, this sideways lift counteracts the main rotor engine's desire to spin the body of the helicopter.

Without a tail rotor, the helicopter would auto-rotate to the ground. The body will spin in the opposite direction of the main rotor until it crashes.

Top view

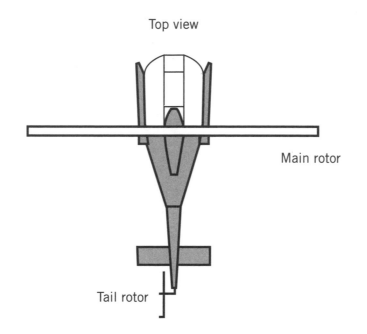

Main rotor

Tail rotor

A helicopter steers and flies by the use of both sets of rotors. Airplanes have a fixed wing—only the flaps and rudders are adjustable. In a helicopter, the entire wing can change its angle. This angle is called the **angle of attack**. Changing the angle of attack can change the direction of the lift. By changing the direction of the lift of both rotors, helicopters can fly in any direction. The main rotor is controlled by the pilot's hands, and the tail rotor is controlled by the pilot's feet.

Now, let's build some helicopters and let them auto-rotate to the ground.

Apache

Launch this high-flying helicopter above the treetops and let it auto-rotate to the ground.

Flight Gear

Pencil or pen
Index card or scrap cardstock
Scissors
Rubber band

Stapler
Clear Tape
Paper clip
Ruler

Step 1: Draw the pattern pictured below on an index card or scrap cardstock. The size is not important; just make it fit the card you have. Try to keep the relative dimensions the same, though. The two rotor blades should be half the width of your paper and go almost half the length. The bottom of the Apache should be split into thirds so it can be folded later.

Step 2: Use the scissors to cut along the solid lines, but do *not* cut the dashed lines. They will be folded later.

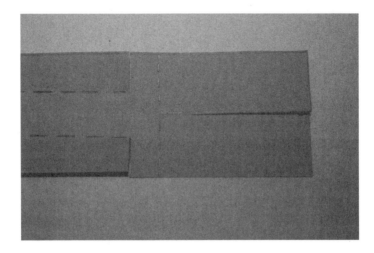

Step 3: Fold each of the outside bottom pieces inward. Before completely folding the bottom, slide a rubber band inside.

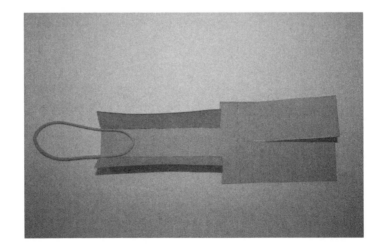

Step 4: Completely fold in the bottom pieces and staple them together. Make sure you "capture" the rubber band but avoid hitting the rubber band with the staple. Pull the rubber band down to make sure it is secure. You can also tape it in place if you don't have a stapler. Adding a paper clip to the bottom can add a little weight and may allow the copter to fly higher. Slide the paper clip up on the bottom pieces.

Step 5: Fold the top wings. One is folded to the right and one is folded to the left. Use your thumb to press down this crease.

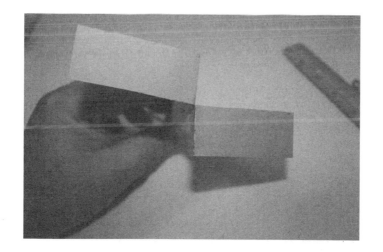

Step 6: The Apache works best outside, unless you have a two-story room or gymnasium. Hook the end of the rubber band to the end of the ruler (or you can use the Straight-as-an-Arrow launcher on page 164). Keep the rotors straight and hold them by the tips. Keeping both hands behind the front of the wings makes it easier to avoid hitting the rotors as the Apache is launched. Pull back the rubber band and let the Apache fly. Aim up in the air for the longest hang time.

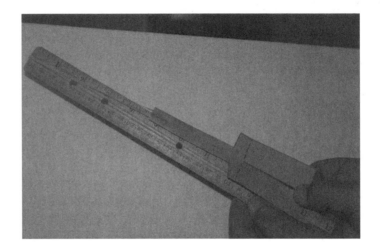

Advanced Flight Topics

Helicopters demonstrate the principle of a rotating wing. Try different launch angles for maximum air time. If you are outside, investigate how the wind helps or hurts the flight path. Also try bending the wings against the bottom as you launch the Apache and see what happens.

Straw Copter

Spin your hands and let the Straw Copter soar into the wild blue yonder.

Flight Gear

Scissors
Scrap paper
Ruler
Pencil
Hole punch
Clear tape
Drinking straw

Step 1: Usc the scissors to cut a 1-inch by 8-inch strip from the scrap paper. Use a pencil to mark the middle of the strip.

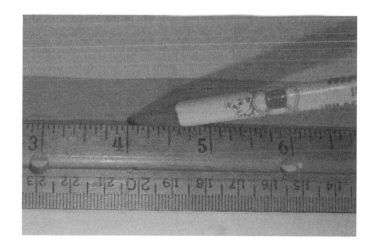

Step 2: Use a hole punch to punch out a hole exactly on the midpoint pencil mark. Draw two lines an equal distance from the center hole. The lines should be on opposite sides of the strip and extend just beyond halfway across the strip, as shown.

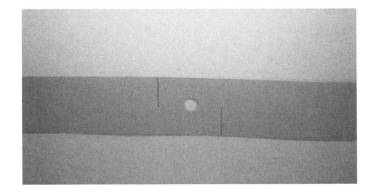

Step 3: Cut each one of the lines you just drew. Fold one side of the rotor but do *not* crease the fold. The curved edge will be leading edge of the airfoil for the rotor. Repeat for the other side's rotor. Secure the folds with a small piece of tape as you are folding them.

Step 4: Tape along the entire back edge of each airfoil. Wrap the tape around both sides and smooth out that edge only. Take care not to crease the other side of the airfoil. You now have two airfoils, one on each side of your rotor.

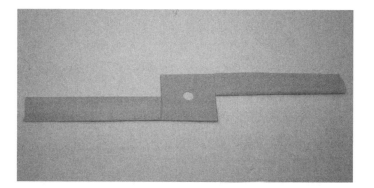

Step 5: Use scissors to cut a slit about ½ inch on one end of a drinking straw. You can cut both sides at the same time if you use your thumb and index finger to slightly flatten the straw first. Slide the cut end of the straw through the hole you punched in the center of your rotor. Fold down the cut halves of the straw, away from each other, and tape it to the top of the rotor. Using two tiny pieces of tape to make an *X* works best.

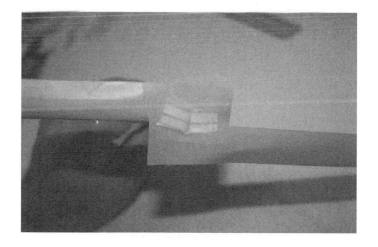

Step 6: Now you are ready to launch. This launch takes some practice to master. Put the bottom of the Straw Copter between your palms. Pull one hand toward your body and push one hand away quickly. This will cause the Straw Copter to spin. You don't have to let go of the Straw Copter, since your hands will separate naturally as you push and pull them. The straw should lift up a little and then rotate to the ground. Make sure the untaped edges of the rotor are spinning as the front edge.

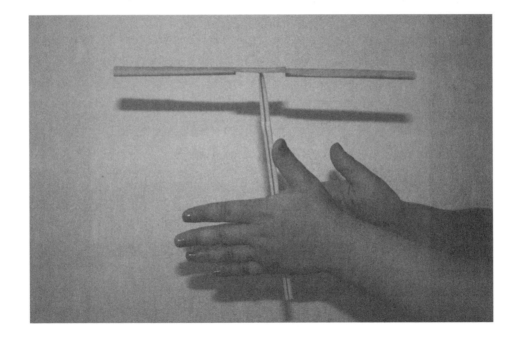

Super Spinner

A spool and some string and are all you need to launch this helicopter to new heights.

Flight Gear

Thin piece of cardboard
Pencil
Ruler
Marker
Empty spool
White glue
String (or shoelace or thread)
Pen or pencil
Scissors

Step 1: Start with a square piece of thin cardboard. The picture below is 8½ inches square, but it could be any size between 6 and 12 inches square. Locate the middle of one side.

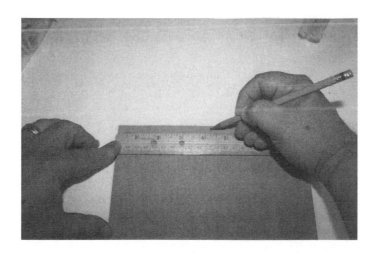

Step 2: Draw an *X* in the center of the entire square sheet of cardboard.

Step 3: Make a *Y* in pencil on the cardboard. To do this, draw a line from the top middle down to the *X*. Now draw a line from each bottom corner up to the *X*. You should have an upside-down pencil *Y* on your cardboard now.

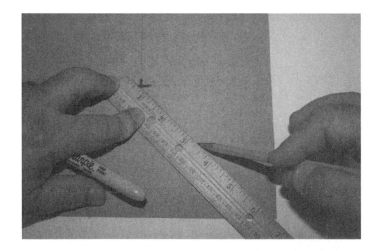

Step 4: Use the ruler to measure from the middle X to the top of the cardboard square. Place a small line on each of the bottom legs at that same distance. You should have three legs that are all equal distance now.

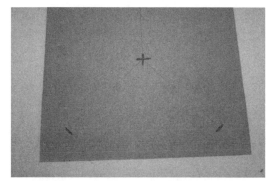

Step 5: Draw an arc from the center X to the end of each leg. An easy way to do this is to put your drawing hand directly between the two points with the pencil slightly extended from normal. Now, starting at one end, draw an arc to the other end. Don't pick up your hand—just let your hand pivot on the cardboard. This will take some practice. (Good thing you are using a pencil.) Repeat for all of the lines on both sides. You should now have a three-bladed flower (see Step 6) in pencil. Use a reverse curve to connect the rotor blades, so there is a solid circle in the center to glue the spool to.

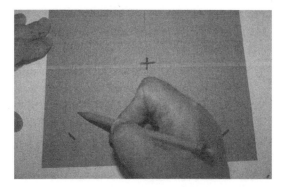

Step 6: Once you are happy with your pencil-drawn flower, you can darken it in with a marker.

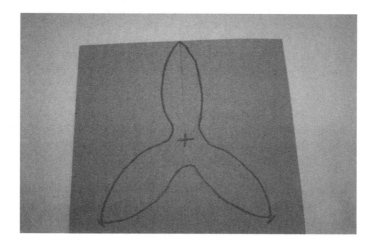

Step 7: Now draw a dotted line along the leading edge of each wing. The picture is drawn for a right-handed thrower. If you are left-handed, draw the dotted lines on the opposite edge of each wing. These dotted lines are going to be folded in the next step. Cut along the dark lines using your scissors.

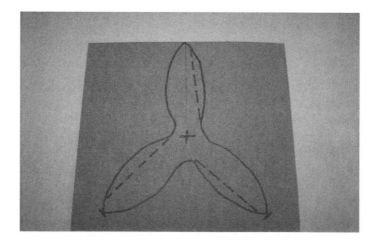

Step 8: Using your thumb and fingers, curve down each rotor blade along the dotted lines. Curve them down about ½ inch. You can always adjust the downward curve later.

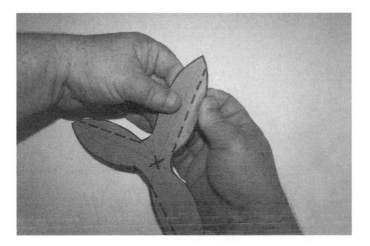

Step 9: Place the spool with the best gluing surface (fewer holes) up. Apply glue and place the spinner atop the center of the spool. Allow the glue to dry completely—at least 1 hour— before going to the next step. You might want to build another flyer while you wait.

Step 10: Now wind a length of string around the bottom of the spool. Wind several times and then lightly pull. The folded-down part of the blades should be in the *rear* as it spins. Once you know which way is correct, wind the string tightly around the spool, keeping it near the bottom.

Step 11: Balance the bottom of the spool on the end of a pen or pencil. Hold it slightly above your head and quickly pull the string.

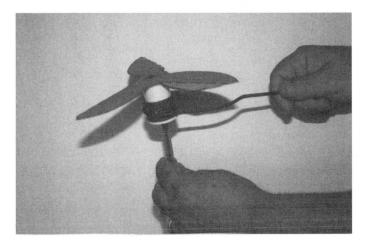

Advanced Flight Topics

Try curving the blades more steeply, or less, to see what gives you maximum helicopter flight time. You might want to try launching the Spinner off a deck or balcony to give it more time to twirl.

Maple Key Helicopter

Create a paper flyer that looks like a maple key (seed) and toss it to watch nature in action.

Flight Gear

Square piece of paper (example shown is 8½ inches square,
    but almost any size will work)

Step 1: The Maple Key Helicopter is tough to fold, but you will eventually master it. Don't get frustrated—at first, it took me three tries to do it right. Start by folding the paper diagonally from corner to corner. Use your thumbnail to press down the crease.

Step 2: Open the fold back up and fold along the same line again, but in reverse. The other side of the paper should now be on the outside. Use your thumbnail again to

press down the crease. All of the folds through Steps 2 and 3 should be done in the same manner. Folding and refolding will make it easier to do some of the later steps.

Step 3: Repeat another fold (and refold) diagonally, connecting the other two corners. Also fold (and refold) from side to side in both directions. The folds you should have when you finish are shown in marker in the photo below.

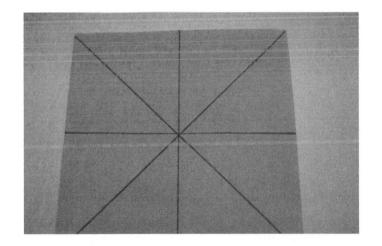

Step 4: Fold two opposite corners into the center, as shown. Use your thumbnail to press down the crease. This fold and the rest of the folds for the Maple Key Helicopter do *not* need to be refolded like before.

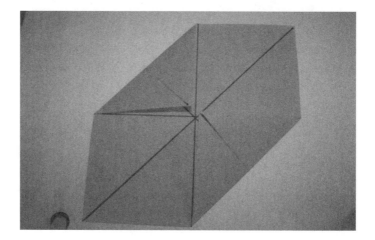

Step 5: Lift the two remaining end corners up toward the top. The points should come together at the top and the two folds should be bent inside, as shown.

Step 6: While holding the top two points together, press the small triangles flat.

Step 7: After Step 6, your flyer should look like this. The folds are pretty flexible, so unfold and try again if it doesn't.

Step 8: Take one outside point and fold in until the point meets the center line. Only fold the top sheet of paper.

Step 9: Repeat Step 8 for the three other points.

Step 10: Take one of the folds you just created and create a valley fold. Fold until the outside of the top sheet reaches the center line.

Step 11: Repeat Step 10 for each of the other three sides.

Step 12: Open up one of the double folds you just created. You should be folding up the top layer only. The bottom layer should stay flat on the table.

Step 13: Turn the flyer over and unfold the other side. Your flyer should look like the picture.

Step 14: Fold the top wing out and over at a 45-degree angle. Try to get the fold all the way through all the layers of the Maple Key Helicopter so your rotors can be large. It will be hard to press the bottom since it is several sheets thick. You can use a ruler or a heavy object to help smooth that fold.

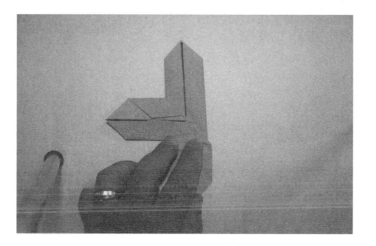

Step 15: Turn over the Maple Key Helicopter and repeat for the other rotor blade. Pick up the flyer by the bottom and bend out the wings slightly.

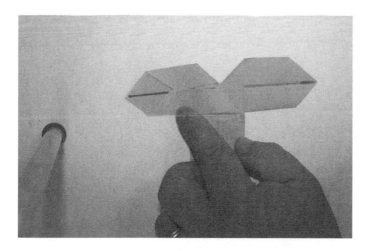

Step 16: Now you are ready to launch. Drop the Maple Key Helicopter from as high as possible and watch it auto-rotate to the ground. You can also try throwing it up in the air instead of dropping it. Go outside for maximum hang time.

Advanced Flight Topics

Try tweaking the angle of the rotors to increase hang time. Go out to the yard (or park) and find a real maple key. Compare it to your flyer. You will notice the maple key is only a single blade with an added weight opposite of the blade. The added weight is actually the maple tree seed.

Fantastic Four-Blade

Aim high as you launch this four-bladed helicopter.

Flight Gear

Scissors
Paper or cardstock
Pencil
Ruler
Clear tape
Paper clips

Step 1: Use the scissors to cut a strip of paper 2½ inches by 8 inches. With the pencil, draw four parallel lines lengthwise that are each ½ inch apart. Plain scrap paper will work, but heavier cardstock will work also.

Step 2: Fold along one of the ½-inch lines and crease with your thumbnail. Unfold the fold you just made. The crease should still be visible. Repeat for all of the other lines. Draw a line across the middle of your strip, 4 inches up from the bottom. Use scissors

to cut along each fold line from the top down to the 4-inch line. Cut off one of the rotor blades at the 4-inch line, as shown.

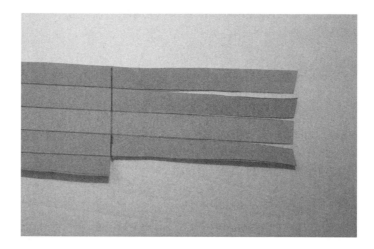

Step 3: Turn the Fantastic Four-Blade over. The pencil marks will go to the inside. Lay the ruler across the 4-inch line. Line the ruler up across the middle and place the edge at the bottom of all four cut lines. You can cut any that don't match up exactly with the ruler now. Start with the right-hand blade and bend it to the right at a 45-degree angle, as shown. Bend the blade down until it lies along the edge of the ruler.

Step 4: Leave the first blade bent over and laying flat. Repeat for all the other blades.

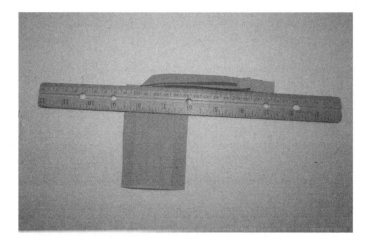

Step 5: Now pick up the Fantastic Four-Blade. Make the body (bottom) fold into a square. Remember you have a fifth piece, without a blade, on the bottom. The fifth piece will tuck inside the square. Use a small piece of tape to secure the top and bottom of the body.

Step 6: Place two paper clips on either side of the body. You can slide these up from the bottom into the square tube of the body.

Step 7: Drop the Fantastic Four-Blade from as high as possible and watch it twirl to the ground. You can also throw it like a dart and watch it twirl up and down. Toss it off a deck or balcony if one is available.

Advanced Flight Topics

Adjust the pitch (angle) of the blades to change the fall time. Try adjusting the weight by adding or removing paper clips at the bottom to change the flight time.

6

Launchers

The science of launchers will be explained in Flight School for this topic. Rubber band–powered launchers will shoot everything from day-old produce to neat, little mini flyers. As in the other chapters, the projects will progress from basic to advanced.

Flight School

All flying machines must get thrust from somewhere. For the flyers in this book, the thrust comes from muscles, rubber bands, or air pressure. But real planes get thrust from other sources.

The simplest source is a propeller. A propeller is just a sideways-mounted wing that is attached to an engine—thank you, Orville and Wilbur Wright. The prop is an airfoil that creates lift. But since it is turned sideways, the lift propels the plane forward instead of up. Standard lift from the wings keeps the plane up, but the prop drives it forward. Propeller-driven planes are very fuel efficient but can only fly at low speeds. There are even human-powered and solar-powered propeller-driven airplanes.

If you want to go faster, you need more power. About 40 years after the Wright brothers' innovations, a new means of propulsion was invented: the jet. A jet engine works by taking air in from the front. This air is then sped up and shot out the back of the engine really, really fast. This fast-moving exhaust gas causes an action and the plane experiences a reaction—the plane speeds up. The faster the gas comes out, the faster the plane flies. The faster the air comes out, the more force you feel. Commercial jets blow out exhaust gas over a long period of time and accelerate slowly up to cruising speed. Military jets blow out exhaust gas very quickly and therefore accelerate quickly. There are different types of jet engines for all purposes.

But now let's propel some flyers.

X-Wing Flyer and Launcher

Use a paper towel tube to create a fun flyer. Pull and aim the X-Wing Flyer at targets across the room.

Flight Gear

Scissors
Drinking straw
Clear tape
Paper clip
Paper towel tube

2 rubber bands
Duct tape
Stapler
Pencil

Step 1: Build the X-Wing first. Use the scissors to cut four 1-inch-long pieces from a drinking straw. To create the engine pods, use clear tape to tape two of the 1-inch pieces together. Repeat for the two remaining 1-inch pieces.

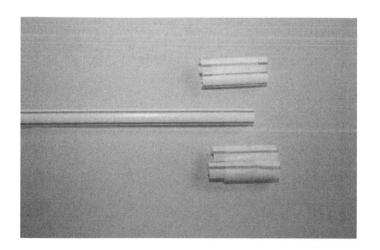

Step 2: Tape one of the pod pairs to a 4-inch-long piece of straw. Extend the pod at least ¼-inch beyond the body of the straw and make sure the tape is near the body end of the pod.

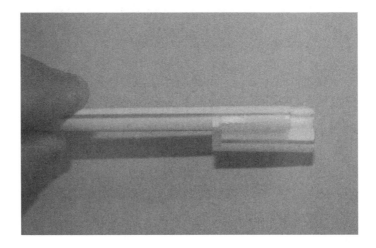

Step 3: Tape the remaining pod to the other side of the body. Again, make sure that the tape is near the front and the pods are on opposite sides of the X-Wing's body, as shown.

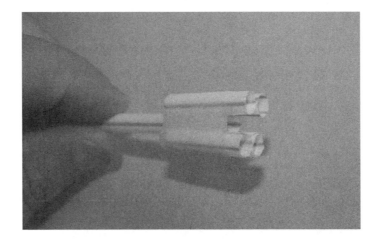

Step 4: Slide the inner loop of a paper clip into the nose of the X-Wing.

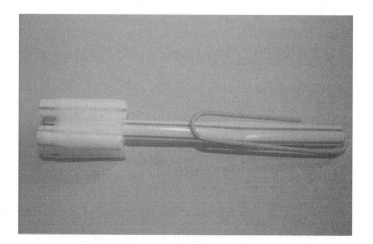

Step 5: Now build the launcher. Cut a ½-inch-wide strip out of the entire length of a paper towel tube.

Step 6: Bend the strip around the center of two rubber bands. Secure the front and back of the paper towel strip with duct tape, staples, or both. This will serve as the trigger for your launcher.

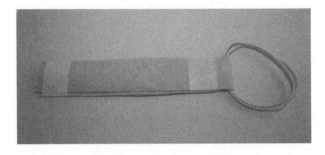

Step 7: Shorten the launcher tube by cutting 2 inches off one end of the tube. Use duct tape to wrap the paper towel tube back into a tube, closing up the gap you made when you removed the strip. Wrapping a center piece first makes it easier to hold together. Tape the entire tube except for 1 inch at one end.

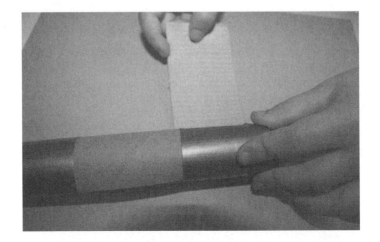

Step 8: Make four cuts equal distance apart around the untaped end of your launcher. Fold down two of the four areas created by the last cuts, as shown. The folded-down

pieces should be on opposite sides of your launcher. Also, do not fold down the piece where the paper towel tube overlaps.

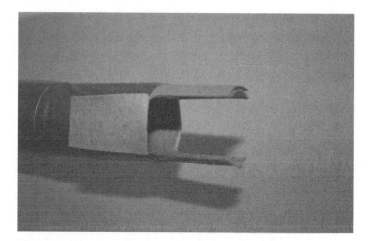

Step 9: Slide the trigger strip inside the launcher tube. The trigger strip should be parallel to the two folded-down pieces of the launcher tube. You might need to trim the trigger strip if it doesn't fit. Trim and use more tape if needed. It should slide smoothly in your launcher tube.

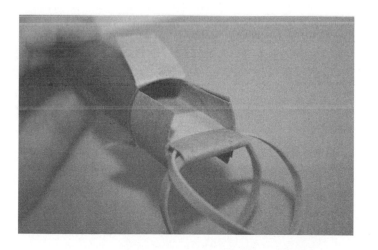

Step 10: Fold the rubber bands to the outside of the folded pieces of the launcher tube. Pull back the trigger strip to tighten the rubber bands. Use a pencil to push the trigger strip down from the front until you can reach it.

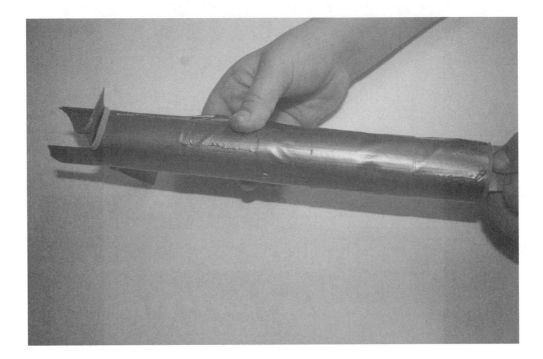

Step 11: Wrap a piece of duct tape around the outside front. Make sure the folded-down pieces are secure and the rubber bands are free to stretch. Cut off the two remaining pieces of the launcher that were never folded down. Your launcher is ready.

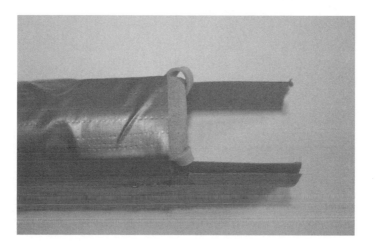

Step 12: Slide the X-Wing into the launcher. Make sure the opening between the pods can be captured by the trigger strip.

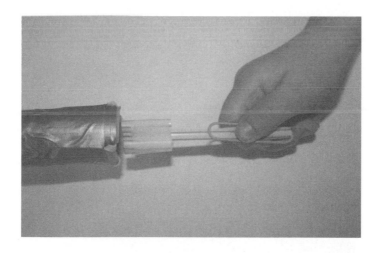

Step 13: The X-Wing Launcher can be dangerous, so take care to aim away from animals, friends, and your Mom's china. Pull back on the trigger strip. Ready. Aim. Fire!

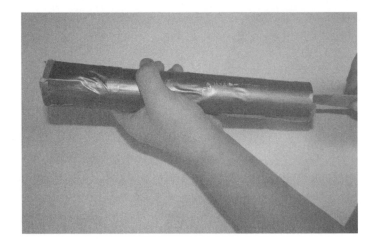

Advanced Flight Topics

Build more X-Wing Launchers to have even more fun. (Let's face it, shooting the X-Wings is more fun than chasing them down.) You also might want to try longer X-Wing Launchers made from two straws.

Grape Bazooka

Shoot grapes over 30 feet with the Grape Bazooka.

Flight Gear

Heavy scrap paper
Pencil
Plastic drink bottle cap
2 rubber bands
Duct tape (or masking tape)

Stapler
Scissors
Paper towel tube (or toilet paper tube)
Ammo (grapes, balls of tape, or
    small Super Balls)

Step 1: Fold a long strip of heavy scrap paper by making ½-inch folds. Keep wrapping the paper around itself until it is all folded. You should end up with a long, narrow piece for your trigger. You can also use lightweight cardboard (like from a cereal box) for this and skip folding.

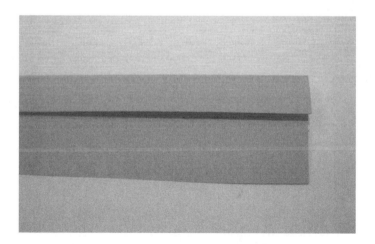

Step 2: Use a pencil to mark the center of the trigger strip. Place the center over an upside-down plastic bottle cap. Place two rubber bands over the bottle cap and under the trigger strip.

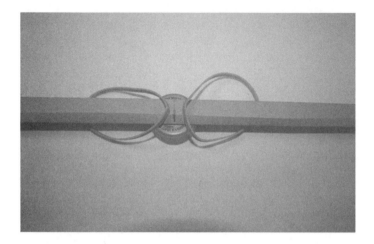

Step 3: Use two tiny pieces of duct tape (or masking tape) to hold the trigger and rubber bands in place. Make sure both the rubber bands and the trigger are secure. You can trim off any excess tape with scissors.

Step 4: Wrap a very thin strip of duct tape around the edge of the bottle cap. Make sure you have captured both rubber bands and the taped parts of the rubber bands have an equal stretch.

Step 5: Fold down both ends of the trigger strip away from the bottle cap. Secure them with tape or staples.

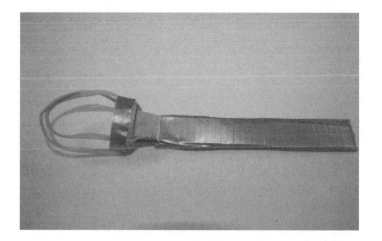

Step 6: Now you are going to attach the cap to the launching tube. Wrap a piece of tape around the paper towel tube 1 inch from the end. Use scissors to make four cuts all

the way to the tape. Here is a trick to make them equal distance: Make one cut to the tape. Cut the exact opposite side next. Make a cut halfway between your first two cuts. Now make a cut on the opposite side of the third cut. Four equal-distance cuts!

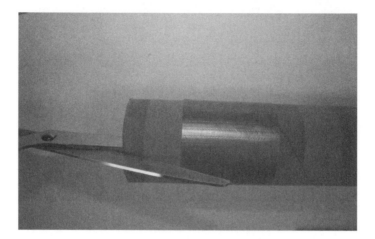

Step 7: Fold down all four areas between the cuts.

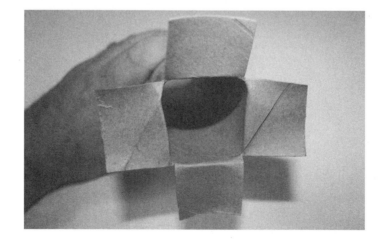

Step 8: Put the cap, with the open side facing out, into the tube. Slide the rubber bands over the two opposite sides that are folded down.

Step 9: Fold the two paper towel tube pieces that are holding the rubber bands in place. Use a piece of tape to secure the folded pieces. Cut off the two remaining pieces flush with the front of your Grape Bazooka.

Step 10: Use scissors to trim the length of the tube down to size, about 6 inches. If you use a toilet paper tube, it will probably not have to be trimmed for length. The length of the Grape Bazooka may vary based on the length of your rubber bands. The trigger

strip should extend just beyond the back end of your Grape Bazooka. Wrap the entire launcher tube in tape for strength.

Step 11: Time to load your Grape Bazooka. Place your ammo in the tube while holding the tube at an angle. Grapes, balls of tape, and small super balls will all work, but don't use anything hard. The picture below shows balled-up scrap paper left over from other flying machine projects.

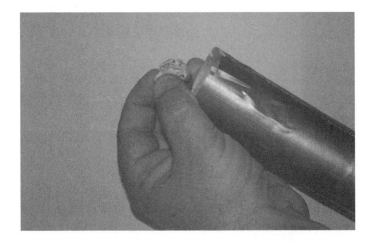

Step 12: Pull back the trigger strip and let it go. One hand should pull while the other holds the tube and aims at the target. Remember, don't aim at friends, enemies, pets, or breakable stuff.

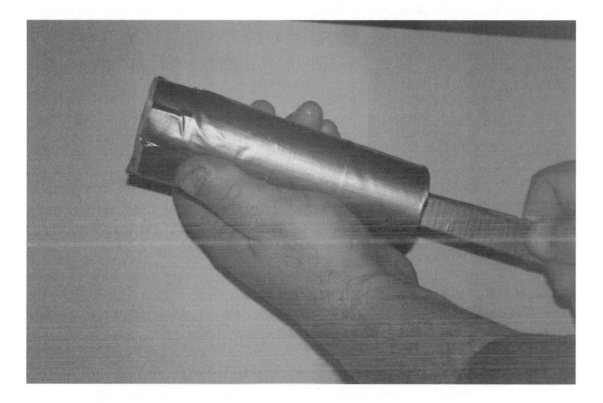

Advanced Flight Topics

Thrust is the key to the Grape Bazooka, so experiment with different pull lengths. Also, vary the launch angle to control how high and how far your projectiles go. Set up a bucket across the yard and try to land your projectiles in the bucket. If you make two launchers, you can challenge a friend and see who gets more ammo into the bucket.

Straight-as-an-Arrow Launcher

You can build this free launcher to shoot your rubber band–powered flyers. Aim for the treetops!

Flight Gear

Piece of cardboard
Scissors
Felt-tip markers or crayons

Step 1: Use the scissors to cut a 1- to 2-inch-wide strip of cardboard, at least 10 inches long. The size can vary a little based on the cardboard you have.

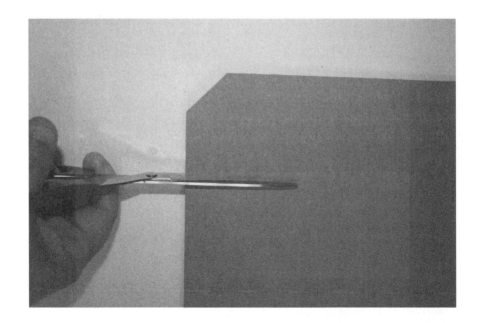

Step 2: Cut a small *V* notch in one end.

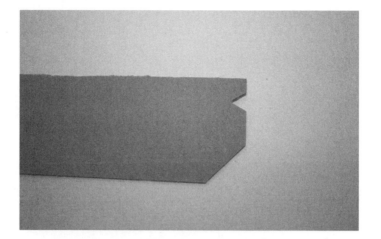

Step 3: Decorate your finished launcher.

Advanced Flight Topics

This device gives you the ability to launch most of the rubber band–powered flyer projects in this book. Most can also be launched with a ruler, but isn't it more fun to launch the flyers with something you made and decorated?

Pistol Grip Launcher

Duct tape and rubber bands create a launcher that shoots your flyers to new heights.
Adult supervision required

Flight Gear

Ruler
Cardboard
Marker
Scissors
Sharp knife
Duct tape (or masking tape)
Thick rubber band

Step 1: Place a ruler in the middle of the piece of cardboard. Trace both sides of the ruler using a marker.

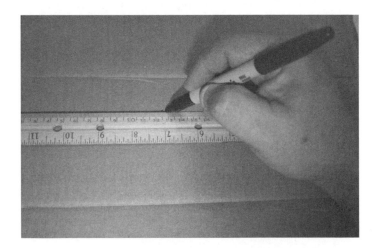

Step 2: Move the ruler to each side of the outline and trace the outside of the ruler again. You should have three spaces, each separated by about 1 inch, the width of the ruler. If you don't have a ruler, draw four lines about 1 inch apart down the center of your cardboard. Also, draw two handles going back at a slight angle, as shown. Make the lines parallel. You can trim them once the cardboard is folded.

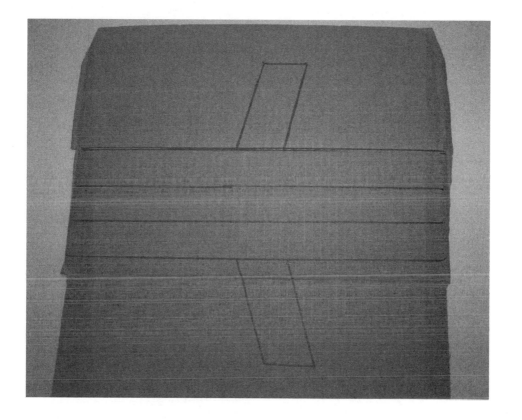

Step 3: Use scissors to cut out around the handles and the three spaces making up the body of your Pistol Grip Launcher.

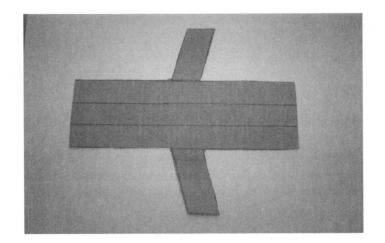

Step 4: Get an adult to help for this part. Use a sharp knife and a ruler to score the inner two lines on your launcher. To score a line it is important that you lightly cut through just one side of the cardboard, but not the backside.

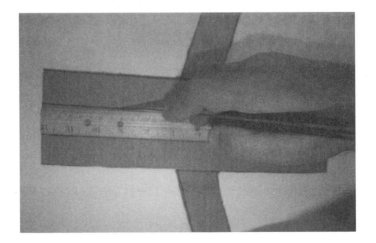

Step 5: Fold the two edge pieces up while the middle stays flat on a hard surface. Temporarily secure the body together with a strip of duct tape at both ends. Masking tape will also work.

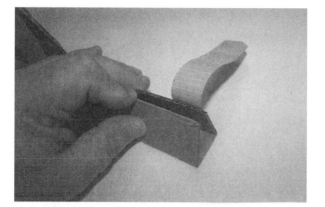

Step 6: Wrap a small strip of tape around the top of the handle, next to the barrel, as shown. You can now trim the pistol grip to fit your hand for width and length. Hold it like a pistol and see what feels comfortable in your hand. Use the scissors to trim it if necessary. If you have to cut the tape, just replace it once the grip has been trimmed to fit your hand. After the handle is right, you can wrap the entire launcher with duct tape for strength.

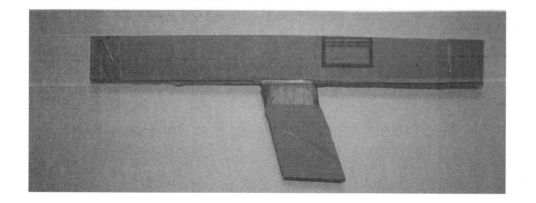

Step 7: Use the scissors to cut the top two corners—the two farthest away from the pistol grip—at the front end of the launcher. Make these cuts about 1 to 1½ inches long and the same length.

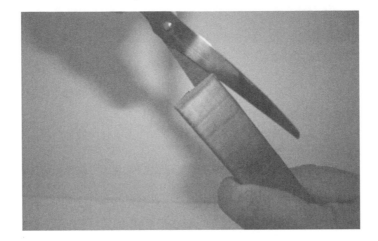

Step 8: Slide the rubber band all the way to the back of these slots. Make sure the rubber band is not twisted.

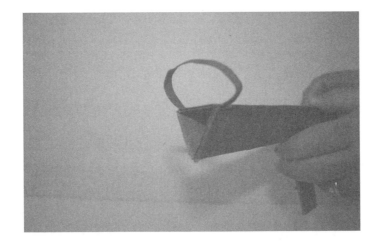

Step 9: Use a strip of duct tape to secure the rubber band inside the Pistol Grip Launcher. Press the strip inside the Launcher and wrap it through the rubber band onto the top of the Launcher.

Step 10: Wrap a strip of duct tape around the body of the Launcher, just behind the rubber band. You can also wrap a thin strip around the body in front of the rubber band. If and when the rubber band breaks, you can replace it by repeating Steps 7, 8, 9, and 10.

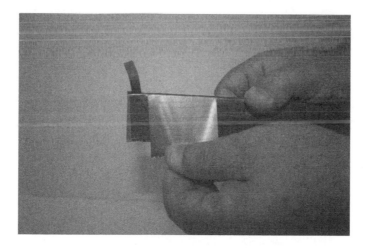

Step 11: Your Pistol Grip Launcher is now complete.

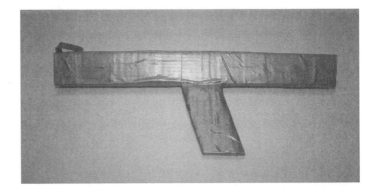

Step 12: Now you are ready to launch many of your flyers. The Pistol Grip Launcher works with any flyers that have a notch cut in the bottom for a rubber band.

Advanced Flight Topics

You can try different rubber bands when the old ones break. Rubber bands of different widths have different strengths.

Pringles Launcher

Launch all types of projectiles toward the stars with this fun recycled launcher.
Adult supervision required

Flight Gear

Scissors or sharp knife

Pringles can (small or large)

Balloon

Duct tape

Ammo (balls of scrap paper, small water balloons, or grapes)

Optional: Can opener

Step 1: Ask an adult to help you cut the Pringles can. Start by cutting one end off a small Pringles can, or make two Pringles Launchers by cutting across the middle of a large can. After cutting, the can should be no more than 4 inches long with one "factory end" still intact. You can use a can opener to cut out the bottom if you are making two Launchers from a tall can.

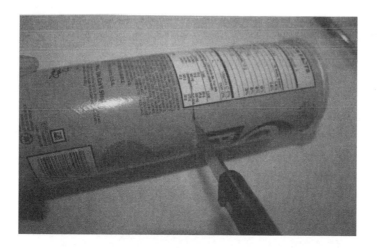

Step 2: Blow up a balloon, then let it go and watch it zip around the room. You have just built the world's simplest rocket. (Real rockets aren't built out of rubber, so they fly a little straighter.) Repeat this three or four times to fully stretch out the balloon. Then, with the balloon deflated, tie a knot in the neck of the balloon like you would do if it was blown up. Finally, cut a small hole in the top of the balloon opposite from the neck.

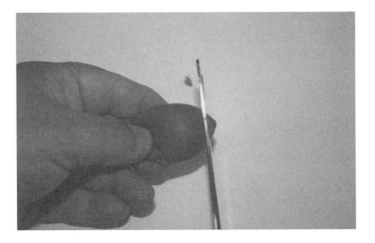

Step 3: Point the balloon's knot down inside the Pringles can. Stretch the hole out and hook it over the smooth "factory edge" of the can. Sometimes an extra set of hands is needed for this part, so enlist the help of a sibling, friend, or parent.

Step 4: Secure the top of the balloon in place with a strip of duct tape. You can cover the rest of the can with duct tape for a space-age look if you want, but it is not needed since the can is pretty strong.

Step 5: Now you are ready to launch your ammo. Balls of scrap paper, small water balloons, grapes, or anything that will fit in a Pringles can is perfect for ammo. Hold the can at an angle to load. Reach in the back with one hand and pull the knot of the balloon. Use the other hand to hold the Pringles Launcher. Ready. Aim. Fire!

Advanced Flight Topics

Try different launch angles. Experiment with different types of ammo and have fun. Launch paper balls (or ping-pong balls) straight up in the air and see if you can catch them.

7

Boomerangs

Master the ancient art of the boomerang with free materials. Boomerang science will be explained in Flight School to demystify the fabulous come-back flyer. Throwing a boomerang is as easy as riding a bike. From tiny Fingerrangs to the large Aussie, boomerangs are fun to throw, catch, and recycle. Also featured will be a neat come-back flyer created from two coffee cups.

Flight School

Boomerangs were probably an accidental discovery based on an old hunting weapon, the hunting stick. Hunting sticks were simply carved bent sticks. Because bent sticks rotate, they fly better than straight sticks. The hunting sticks were thrown at small game animals. The heavy bent sticks would knock the animal out when it hit (if the hunter was lucky). The Aborigines in Australia are credited with discovering the boomerang. They used a larger version called a *kylie* for hunting. The *kylie* was thrown overhand like a baseball but did not return. That is a good thing, since it was heavy and designed to hurt people or animals. By accident or through experiments, Aborigines discovered that a smaller version of the *kylie* would curve when thrown, and the returning boomerang was born. Boomerangs are not very good hunting tools, however, since they curve as they fly.

Two science principles cause the boomerang's crazy curve: lift and gyroscopic precession. Traditional boomerangs are just two wings joined at the middle. Since they are shaped like an airfoil, the wings experience lift as the boomerang spins. Lift is explained by the Bernoulli principle. Boomerangs are thrown almost vertically, so the lift is horizontal to the ground. The top wing feels a greater lift than the bottom wing since it is spinning 'into' the air. Spinning into the air causes more air to be moved around the top wing and a greater lift. The bottom wing is spinning out of the air (and moves less air), so it feels less lift.

Since the lift on the top wing causes the boomerang to lean inward, it will curve due to gyroscopic precession. A similar example is a spinning top. As the top leans in, it will move in a circle around the axis. Rolling a coin also results in the same curve. Learning to throw a boomerang (or flicking a Fingerrang) takes a lot of practice. Eventually, you will get it to curve back to you.

Boomerangs come in all shapes and sizes. Now, you can make your own and fling away.

Basic Fingerrang

Just a flick of your finger launches this fun-to-fly Basic Fingerrang.

Flight Gear

Pencil
Old greeting card (or any scrap piece of cardstock)
Scissors
Book (or flat surface)

Step 1: Use a pencil to draw a *V* on one side of the greeting card. If your card has a nice picture, draw the *V* on the backside. Try to make the *V* about 3 inches from point to point, across the top. The Fingerrang should be no wider than your palm. After you build a few of these, you can probably skip drawing the Fingerrang pattern.

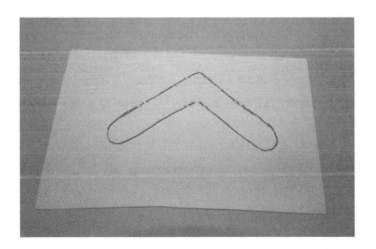

Step 2: Use scissors to cut out the Fingerrang pattern. Keep the scraps.

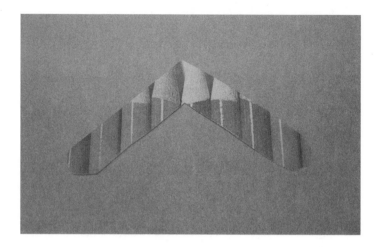

Step 3: Using both hands, slightly bend up one corner of the Fingerrang.

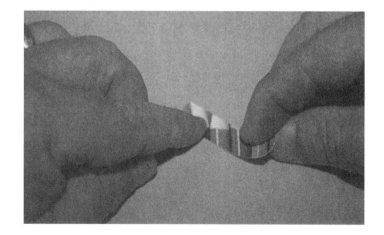

Step 4: Place the Fingerrang on the edge of a flat surface—a book works well. Bend your finger back into the flicking position. Flick your finger and strike one end of the Fingerrang to watch it fly. Repeat until you can get the Fingerrang to curve back to you. With practice, you can get rid of the book and just place the Fingerrang on the back of your fist to flick it.

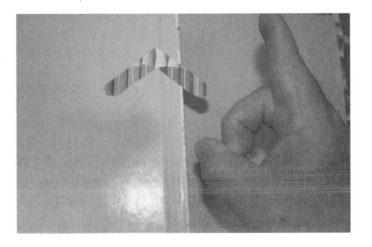

Advanced Flight Topics

Spin speed and the angle of attack are keys for a long Fingerrang flight. Try using different fingers to find the one that works best. Launch your Fingerrang at several angles to get the best flight trajectory.

You can change the angle of the book in two dimensions. A right-to-left tilt will change the curve of the Fingerrang. A front-to-back tilt changes the steepness of the flight. Going outside and taking advantage of the wind is also tons of fun. Realize the wind can help or hurt your flight path, so you will have to experiment to get the best results.

Triple Threat

Toss or flick this three-bladed fingerrang across the room and right back to you.

Flight Gear

Marker
Scrap cardstock (old greeting card, cereal box, etc.)
Scissors
Book

Step 1: Use the marker to draw a *Y* pattern on your cardstock. Each leg of the *Y* should be separated by approximately the same angle. Each leg should be about the width of your index finger but about as long as your pinky. Draw the pattern on the back if you have a cool-looking picture on the front of your cardstock.

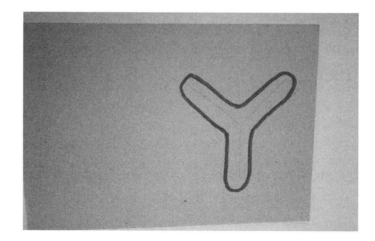

Step 2: Use scissors to cut out the pattern. Using both hands like in the Basic Fingerrang project, slightly bend up one wingtip up.

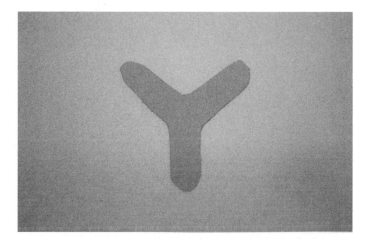

Step 3: Place the Triple Threat on the edge of a book and let one leg hang over the edge. Flick the wingtip and watch it fly. Again, with practice you can eventually launch the Triple Threat off the back of your hand. Try different launch angles until you can get it to "return to sender."

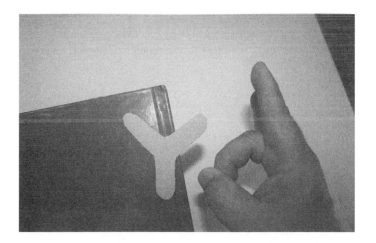

Advanced Flight Topics

Since these are easy to make, make an entire air force of Triple Threats. Try curved wings and angled wings. Try bending all three wingtips and see what happens. You can bend them all up, all down, or two up and one down.

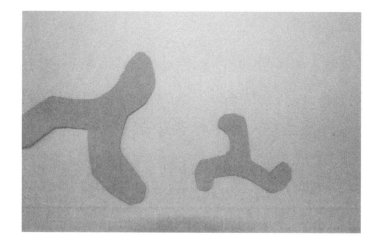

Criss-Cross Flyer

Throw this four-bladed boomerang and watch it curve back to you.

Flight Gear

Scissors
Cereal box or old file folder
Rubber band

Step 1: Use the scissors to cut two 1-inch-wide strips across the width of an old cereal box or an old file folder. Bend the ends of each strip at a right angle about ½ inch from the end.

Step 2: Slip a rubber band around one of the wings. Lay the other wing on top of it near one end, as shown.

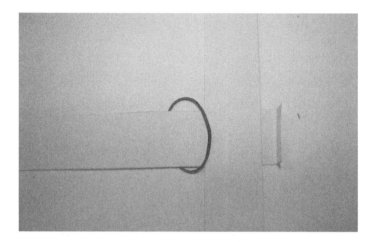

Step 3: Pick up the rubber band and twist it once so that it forms an *X*. Slide the other loop of the rubber band over the top wing and around the other end of the bottom wing. You should have an *X* on top of your two wings.

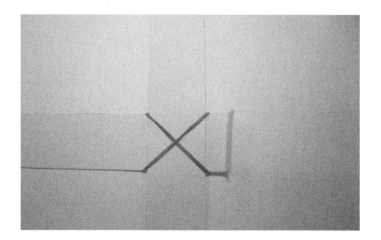

Step 4: Now slide the top wing until the wings make a large X and the rubber band makes a small X.

Step 5: Now you are ready to throw your Criss-Cross Flyer. Grab it between your thumb and forefinger, as shown. Throw it forward from over your shoulder by flicking your wrist. Adjust the angle until it comes back to you.

Advanced Flight Topics

Try throwing the Criss-Cross Flyer with the winglets (bent wingtips) to the right or left to see if that makes a difference. You can also make this flyer with corrugated cardboard for more weight. Cardboard Criss-Cross Flyers will travel a greater distance because of inertia, so they should only be thrown outside.

Ninja Star

Imagine being a Ninja as you throw this safe, fun, throwing star that you made yourself.

Flight Gear

Pencil or pen
Penny
Cereal box, old file folder, or other thin cardboard
Scissors
Felt-tip markers or crayons
Clear tape or stapler

Step 1: Use a pencil or pen to trace around a penny on a sheet of thin cardboard. Draw and cut out a four-sided star as shown in the picture. Be careful to leave cardboard around the penny. Round the points of the star for safety.

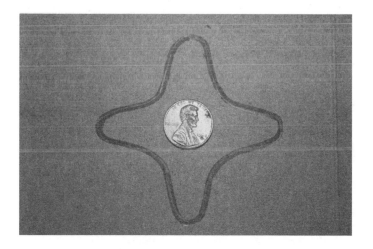

Step 2: Trace your completed star onto another piece of cardboard. Cut out your second star. Now is the perfect time to decorate your stars. If the other side of your cardboard looks good, just put that to the outside.

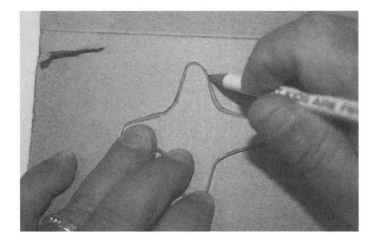

Step 3: Place the penny in the center of one star. Use tape (or staples) to secure the top star to the bottom star. The penny should be trapped between the two stars. Small pieces of tape are the easiest to use.

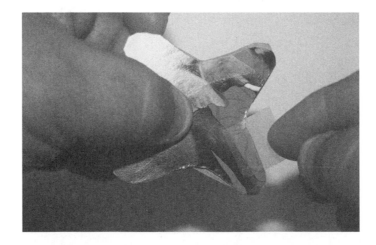

Step 4: Now you are ready to throw the Ninja Star, but remember: never aim at people, pets, or breakable stuff. There are several ways to throw the Ninja Star. You can hold it between your thumb and forefinger and throw it overhead like a baseball. You can also throw it sidearm like a baseball.

Or try this way for a new way to toss things: Put one tip of the star between your first two fingers on your dominant hand. The Ninja Star should be on the inside of your fingers toward your palm. Smash the back of the star hand into the palm of your other hand. This will cause your throwing hand to stop and the Ninja Star will soar toward your target.

Advanced Flight Topics

Try curving up one point of the star and see what happens as you throw it. Technically, Ninja Stars aren't boomerangs. That's good—after all, would you want a Ninja Star to come flying back at you? Of course your Ninja Stars are perfectly safe, and you can get them to curve with a bend in the point.

Aussie

Toss this large three-bladed boomerang and watch it come right back to you.

Flight Gear

Thin cardboard
Pencil
Marker
Ruler
Scissors

Note: If you built the Super Spinner earlier in this book (page 127), the first eight steps below will look familiar—the three-blade wing is exactly the same. However, in this flyer it's used as a boomerang rather than a helicopter.

Step 1: Start with a square piece of thin cardboard. The picture below is 8½ inches square, but it could be any size between 6 and 12 inches square. Locate the middle of one side.

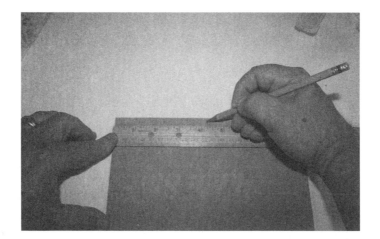

Step 2: With the pencil, draw an *X* in the center of the square sheet of cardboard.

Step 3: Make a *Y* in pencil on your cardboard. Draw a line from the top middle down to the *X*. Now draw a line from each bottom corner up to the *X*. You should have an upside-down pencil *Y* on your cardboard now.

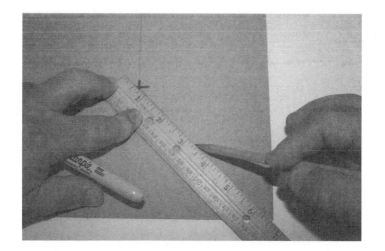

Step 4: Measure from the middle X to the top of the cardboard square. Place a small line on each of the bottom legs at that same distance. You should now have three legs that are all equal distance.

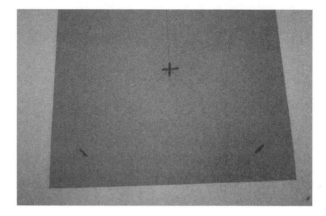

Step 5: Draw an arc from the center X to the end of each leg. An easy way to do this is to put your drawing hand directly between the two points with the pencil slightly extended from normal. Now starting at one end, draw an arc to the other end. Don't pick up your hand—just let your hand pivot on the cardboard. This will take some practice. (Good thing you are using a pencil.) Repeat for all of the lines on both sides. You should now have a three-bladed flower (see Step 6) in pencil.

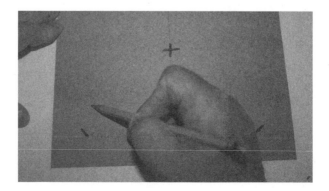

Step 6: Once you are happy with your pencil-drawn flower, you can darken it in with a marker.

Step 7: Now draw a dotted line along the leading edge of each wing. The picture is drawn for a right-handed thrower. If you are left-handed, draw the dotted lines on the opposite edge of each wing. These dotted lines are going to be folded in the next step. Use the scissors to cut along the solid lines.

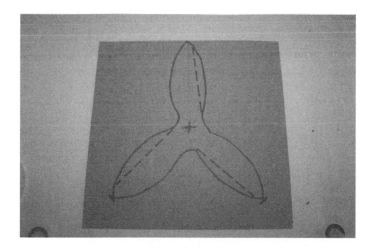

Step 8: Using your thumb and fingers, curve down each rotor blade along the dotted lines. Curve them down about ½ inch. You can always adjust the downward curve later.

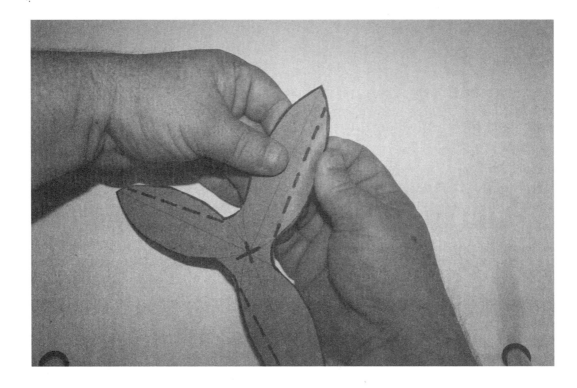

Step 9: Now you are ready to throw the Aussie. Pinch the bottom of one of the blades between your thumb and index finger. Boomerangs are thrown forward from an almost vertical position over your shoulder. It takes a lot of practice to get a boomer-

ang to return to you. Make sure you flick your wrist forward to get maximum spin. Adjust the angle at which you throw the Aussie until it comes back to you.

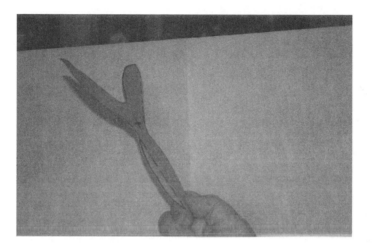

Advanced Flight Topics

Different size boomerangs curve back from different distances. So build a few and vary your sizes. Build a thicker one out of corrugated cardboard, though it may be more difficult to fly. You can also try layering a smaller one on a larger one to get it to curve more.

Also available from Chicago Review Press

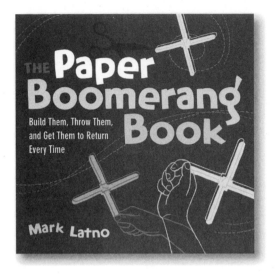

The Paper Boomerang Book

Build Them, Throw Them, and Get Them to Return Every Time

Mark Latno

978-1-56976-282-0
$12.95 (CAN $13.95)

When it comes to lightweight avionics, there's no beating a paper boomerang! Let all the others chase after their folded airplanes—you can now build a flying device that comes right back to you, *every time*. And unlike expensive, heavy wooden boomerangs, paper boomerangs won't endanger windows and skulls.

The Paper Boomerang Book is the first-of-its-kind guide to this fascinating toy. Expert Mark Latno not only tells you how to build but also how to perfect and troubleshoot your own model. Once you've mastered the basic throw, return, and catch, it's on to more impressive tricks—the Over-the-Shoulder Throw, the Boomerang Juggle, the Under-the-Leg Catch, and the dreaded Double-Handed, Backward, Double-Boomerang Throw. And best of all, you don't have to wait for a clear, sunny day to test your flyers—they can be flown indoors in almost any sized room, rain or shine.

Available at your favorite bookstore, by calling (800) 888-4741, or at www.chicagoreviewpress.com

CHICAGO
REVIEW
PRESS